SHAPING
SPIRITUAL LEADERS

Supervision
and Formation in
Congregations

SHAPING SPIRITUAL LEADERS

Supervision and Formation in Congregations

Abigail Johnson

Foreword by Dudley C. Rose

THE
ALBAN
INSTITUTE

Herndon, Virginia
www.alban.org

The Alban Institute
2121 Cooperative Way, Suite 100
Herndon, VA 20171-5370

Unless otherwise noted, all Scripture quotations are from the New Revised Standard Version of the Bible, copyright © 1989, Division of Christian Education of the National Council of the Churches of Christ in the United States of America, and are used by permission.

Cover photo by Michael Lentoft.

Library of Congress Cataloging-in-Publication Data

Johnson, Abigail.
  Shaping spiritual leaders : supervision and formation in congregations / Abigail Johnson.
      p. cm.
  Includes bibliographical references.
  ISBN 978-1-56699-350-0
  1. Christian leadership. 2. Supervision of employees. 3. Church administration. I. Title.

  BV652.1.J635 2007
  253–dc22

                            2007019861

        11   10   09   08   07   VG   1   2   3   4   5

CONTENTS

FOREWORD

A colleague of mine, Elisabeth Schüssler Fiorenza, troubles over the title of pastor, which she derisively says as *herr pastor*. Her concern, as one might guess, has to do with the hierarchical privilege, deference, and power given to or assumed by the clergy. Whether such worry comports with the real situation many churches and denominations currently find themselves in, it does raise a theological point. What is the right role of the pastor?

Ordaining boards ask their aspiring ministers the question in an only slightly different manner. Why be ordained? It is a trick question. The fully egalitarian answer that there is no special difference or role for the ordained minister will furrow the brow of those who grant the office and cause them to withhold the rite. On the other hand, to draw the distinction along lines of power, privilege, or knowledge is to meet a similar end. The wise may choose to quote 1 Corinthians, "And God has appointed in the church first apostles, second prophets, third teachers, then miracles, then gifts of healing, helping, administrating, and various kinds of tongues" (1 Cor 12:28), but they have but begged the same questions.

In the end many denominations and hopeful candidates settle on a modest proposal. Ordination is granted for the purpose of serving the sacraments, they say. The answer is safe enough. The authority it claims for the minister threatens few theological or other decisions in the life of the church. Nonetheless, it grants a particular and different role for the pastor. The answer, it seems, sails successfully between Scylla and Charybdis.

The trouble is, I doubt anyone really believes it. That is, in the Protestant churches, most denominations require no fewer than three years of masters level study as preparation for ordination. Harvard, where I teach, was ostensibly founded in 1636 to assure a "learned clergy." It is a mission that the Divinity School inherited and still embraces. No one I know believes that the three-year course of studies in divinity schools and seminaries is designed principally to prepare one to serve the sacraments.

A more daring claim for the ordained minister's role has been that of resident theologian. Here theological education required for ministry is taken seriously. The seminarian studies Bible and church history, theology and ethics, pastoral care and polity, and more. Together they are the topic set that the minister requires in order to teach and preach theology to the congregation and in some cases beyond. As the resident theologian the minister is educated in much the same way that a doctor or a lawyer or a professor is. The minister has specialized knowledge and training with which to address the theological conundrums of parishioners and even society.

It would be hard to miss the fact that the resident theologian role for the minister fails to escape the criticisms made of *herr pastor*. The resident theologian theologically interprets the world for church and parishioner. The resident theologian preaches, teaches, and prays to and on behalf of the congregation. The resident theologian, like the trained physician, does for laity what the laity has not the wherewithal to do for itself. In the end, the resident theologian model suffers fatal flaws. While performing one's own brain surgery is unreasonable, using one's own brain to grapple with what life throws and to discover a theological interpretation of it are among the most important reasons that people turn to religion. In that light, the role of the ordained minister may at once command less territory than the term resident theologian implies and require a greater complex of skills and capacities.

Abigail Johnson has written a wonderful book that grasps the scope of the project. The title, *Shaping Spiritual Leaders: Supervision and Formation in Congregations*, puts us on notice that the spiritual leaders she has in mind are the members of the congregations, not just their ministers. The job of ministry, then, is less about being a resident theologian than about making theologians and leaders in the community. The mixture of necessary skills is awe inspiring. If ministers are not like surgeons (performing their art on their patients), they must nonetheless know something. One added dimension is that they must also be adept at helping others learn the skills. Another complication is that doing theology is like operating on a moving, changing organism. Consequently, learning to do theology is a dynamic enterprise.

Early in the book, Abigail Johnson gives us a useful metaphor of canoeing in a swift-moving river. She talks about the skill of reading the river. Sometimes you need to go with its currents, sometimes across or against them. What I find most interesting in this analogy is that there are not pat rules and answers to apply to canoeing the river. Two situations may look superficially identical but require entirely different strategies. Think of the minister and a congregant as paddlers. The we're-all-the-same egalitarian minister is likely to get them both killed. The resident theologian minister will take responsibility for reading the river and greatly impress the congregant. But the minister Johnson has in mind will take responsibility as one who has learned to read a river and whose job it is to help the congregant learn to do the same.

The implications are breathtaking. Remember, the river is always changing. No two situations on any river are exactly alike. Similar-looking situations often require entirely different approaches. Learning to read the river is incredibly complicated. It requires both a guide and a teacher for every canoe. What more effective way could there be to get more canoes successfully through the river than to make every paddler a reader of rivers?

Abigail Johnson understands leadership, both that of clergy and laity, as the ability to read and navigate the currents. While many would agree with her, I know of few if any books that guide ministers in their guiding and teaching. Relying on years of work in theological field education, which has long understood the value of reading and navigating contexts, Johnson has authored a book that can best be described as a companion. Through brief case studies, good theory, and lucid prose she walks alongside those who, as teachers and supervisors, would help others become spiritual leaders. Those who accept her invitation will experience the increase in spiritual leadership in the community become geometric. The ride down the river won't be without some splashing water or even a good dose of fear, but those communities that learn to be readers of rivers experience new and wondrous adventures.

Dudley C. Rose
Associate Dean for Ministry Studies
Harvard Divinity School

PREFACE

Through years of supervising field-education students and interns, and in my teaching of those who participated in courses to become supervisors, I have found insights into ways to enrich my ministry leadership through the notion of congregational life as a locus for learning. I view the congregation as a unique learning environment, first because it is perhaps the only community gathering where learning can take place across the generations, where we can learn just as much from a 3-year-old as from a 50-year-old or an 80-year-old. Second, this gathering of people is bound by faith in God, as a spirit who calls us beyond ourselves to serve others with compassion, and as a gift of grace that redeems us and invites us to reach greater potential for Christian discipleship and leadership.

In writing this book I am sharing ways in which I exercised leadership by encouraging the learning of others, both theological students and congregation members. Learning is focused through the development of learning goals, and learning is explored through a covenanted supervisory relationship. Chapter 1 introduces the concept of supervision in congregational life through an imaginary Cross Street United Church. Since leadership development is the purpose of learning and supervision, chapter 2 examines concepts of leadership in congregational life. A great deal has been written about adult learning within the educational field, so in chapter 3 I have drawn on wisdom from adult educators to reflect on learning within a faith community. Chapters 4 and 5 look at the stumbling blocks to learning that arise through conflict and use of power. Chapter 6 covers the nuts and bolts of the supervisory relationship by looking at the learning covenant, the learning goals, the position description, conflict-resolution guidelines, and a process for covenanting with supervisees. Feedback, reflection, evaluation, and closure are all important elements in a learning process as outlined in chapter 7. Finally, chapter 8 offers some brief reflections on the place of spirituality in supervision and learning.

My own learning and leadership development owe a great deal to all those students and congregation members who engaged in learning along with me as we sought to live our faith in word and action.

ONE

SUPERVISION IN A CONGREGATION

For more than 15 years I have been involved with supervising student ministers and training those who wish to become supervisors of student ministers. In my experience, supervision is a process designed to encourage the formation of those who are candidates for ordination within the United Church of Canada.

Supervision involves mentoring a candidate during an internship, a full-time ministry position carried out as part of his or her theological studies. This type of supervision begins with developing a learning covenant that outlines learning goals for both the supervisor and candidate, or supervisee. Weekly supervisory conversations offer opportunities to unpack learning that is taking place and in particular to deepen learning through theological reflection. All this learning is part of the preparation for ordination.

Supervision training, for those who feel called to supervise a candidate for ministry, involves an intensive course addressing such key areas as the learning focus and covenant, conflict, power and authority, learning styles, leadership, supervisory conversations, theological reflection, intimacy and sexuality, feedback and evaluation, and celebration and closure. These key areas focus on issues that may arise in supervision as learning unfolds for a candidate in a congregational setting.

I believe that the notion of supervision is not exclusive to the minister-student relationship. I have found that within congregational ministry, supervision takes place with staff members and key lay leaders as a way to offer support and accountability for their ministry positions. In addition, staff members and lay leaders often supervise others, such as committee members or other staff. Such supervision enhances the vocation of ministry for all concerned.

Generally, I find that supervision is not explicitly addressed in congregational life. Usually supervision is assumed to be part of general planning and pastoral support. However, supervision requires attention to a number of key areas to encourage those supervised to develop their leadership gifts. Supervision can be every bit as important in the formation of lay leaders as in the life of a candidate for ordination.

Formation for Leadership

Formation for ordination is a principal focus of theological schools and church judicatories as they prepare men and women for congregational leadership. This formation includes academic courses in such disciplines as Bible, theology, pastoral care, preaching, worship, church history, and ethics. In addition to taking academic courses, candidates are assigned to congregational placements, where they practice skills for ministry such as preaching, worship leadership, pastoral visiting, administration, and Christian education. Some candidates have further opportunities to learn through a chaplaincy position offered in a clinical pastoral education unit or through spiritual direction. Formation for leadership is taken seriously for those who are seeking ordination.

Unfortunately, formation other than for ordination is not taken as seriously in congregational life. I believe that God calls us into relationship, to be partners in creation throughout our lives and through all our actions and words within the church and in the world. This call is given to all people of God, not simply to a chosen few who become ordained. Ordination is a valued and valuable response to God's call, but it is not the only response. All congregation members are called to discipleship, yet often they are not encouraged, supported, covenanted, educated, or formed for service in the church and world. Interestingly, the Church of Scotland has a service called "ordination" for those in their congregations who become elders, thus expressing the importance placed on lay leadership. A preparation course explores call to ministry and outlines the responsibilities of the position as part of a process to discern this lifelong calling. I would love to see other denominations take the call to lay leadership so seriously.

My understanding of ordination is that it is the church's recognition of a call by God to serve the church—a recognition manifested by supporting the call of each member, sometimes referred to as "equipping the saints" of Christ's church. My response to God as an ordained person is to enliven all God's people to claim and live their call more fully. Throughout my time as a congregational minister, I found myself drawing on the supervisory skills I had learned to encourage the leadership formation of congregation members. These supervisory skills framed my notions of leadership—both my own and those of key lay leaders. Whether you are a minister or key lay leader, however, supervision is an essential process of formation for leadership.

What's in a Name?

Bill, an ordained minister with 27 years' experience, has served three very different congregations—a multipoint rural charge, a downtown inner-city ministry, and currently a suburban program church, Cross Street United. Bill enjoys new challenges and an active ministry. For a number of years he supervised interns, students from the local seminary. He loved the opportunity to work with people new to congregational leadership who brought the latest ideas from theology and Bible studies, as well as congregational studies. The congregation Bill serves is thriving, with many programs for congregation members such as small-group ministries, classes for new Christians, a lectionary reflection group, and a "film and faith" group. This congregation also has a long history of outreach in the community, with programs housed in the church building as well as commitments locally and globally. For instance, the youth group has assisted the local food bank with its food drives three times a year, the outreach committee supported a refugee family for three years after their arrival in the community, and an energetic group has traveled annually to various areas of the globe (for example, Guatemala) to build housing with Habitat for Humanity.

Bill loves the energy in the congregation and has learned to depend on leadership from mature and committed church members to sustain this dynamic ministry. He has found that his training and experience in supervising student pastors has been valuable in his relationship with church leaders. He recognizes that few of these leaders have any particular training in supervision, though they bring willingness to serve and an interest in particular areas of church life.

For quite some time, Bill had wondered how he might pass on some of the wisdom and experience he had gained from supervising interns to the lay leaders who often oversee the work of others in the congregation. In the past year, the chair of the board has been in conflict with the chair of the outreach committee. Although they share similar visions of church outreach, they take very different approaches. Bill has been coaching them in conflict management and reflecting with them about the differences in their styles of leadership. In addition, the youth pastor is an enthusiastic leader, but Bill noticed that this young pastor was unsure how to set clear expectations for youth leaders who have lots of ideas but very little follow-through. Again, Bill found himself coaching the youth pastor on how to supervise the youth leaders. Recently, Bill had a conversation with the chair of worship, Deirdre. She needed to give feedback of a sensitive nature to the church organist, but she was nervous and unsure how to go about this task. Deirdre and Bill discussed various ways to give positive and constructive feedback. From these and similar experiences, Bill began to consider offering training in supervision for congregation leaders to assist them in their work in the church.

Bill finally decided to raise at the next board meeting the possibility of offering a supervision course for congregation leaders. He was surprised when a number of people objected. Deirdre responded, "I'm not a supervisor. I love my work on the worship committee, but I don't see myself telling people what to do." Winston, the youth pastor, agreed, declaring that he didn't want that kind of power and regarded it as more the work of the senior minister to supervise people. However, Wilma, the chair of the board, was excited at the possibility of learning more about how to supervise others in leadership, how to set clear boundaries for positions on committees, and how to be a responsible and accountable leader. The chair suggested that the board discuss the topic further at the next meeting.

Thinking the next day about the board meeting, Bill wrestled with the negative responses to his suggestion. He realized that the term "supervisor" has many meanings. For some, a supervisor is someone with clear authority to hire and fire people, to evaluate and discipline. Perhaps people at the board meeting were reacting to their previous experiences of being supervised, experiences that were negative or unwelcome.

Bill remembered that in the supervision course he took many years ago, people had similar reactions to the word "supervisor." One evening, course participants had an energetic discussion about using a word other than supervisor, such as "mentor" or "coach." What followed were stories about coaches people had worked with, some who were wonderful and others who were miserable and demanding. One woman, recalling a minister trying to "mentor" her, said she had felt manipulated, whereas someone else remembered a friend of the family who had been a profound influence and mentor in her life. After much discussion, people realized that whatever word was used, there would be pros and cons, depending on their experiences. Each word would have positive and negative connotations. Any word would need definition and clarification.

As people related positive and negative experiences of being supervised, a clearer picture unfolded of what a supervisor's role might be. The group did some brainstorming about the word "supervisor" and came up with a number of meanings for the word. At various times, a supervisor may function as mentor, friend, colleague, model, coach, consultant and co-learner, advisor, counselor, guide, teacher, guru, instructor, boss, or manager, depending on the role, the individuals involved, and the situation. Someone asked whether supervision in a church setting is different from that in other settings. Although the church may use information and wisdom from such contexts as education, business, science, and the humanities, a Christian community brings a faith perspective. However imperfectly it is carried out, a Christian community should offer supervision consistent with God's call to love self and neighbor while being faithful to God's vision of abundant life for the world, as expressed in the mission of each congregation. Supervision is an intentional relationship between supervisor and supervisee within a faith community, a relationship in which support and accountability to God's call can be encouraged and enhanced.

The word "intentional" was used several times in the discussion and during the course. Thinking back, Bill appreciated this emphasis. As he thought about his supervision of student ministers, he realized that he brought clear intention to the relationship. The student brought a desire to learn alongside the congregation and Bill. The wider church and seminary organized and supported this learning relationship, expecting a learning congregation committed to the student, a student focused on the learning goals, and a supervisor dedicated to the learning process. The congregation expected to support and encourage student ministers and was prepared to give constructive feedback to help their learning. Clear intention was an important dynamic for all participants in this learning relationship.

As Bill reflected, he realized that lay leaders were not clear about the kinds of relationships they had with others on their committees. Without position descriptions and directions for offering leadership to a committee, lay leaders were left to assume responsibilities as they saw fit. Some lay leaders naturally assumed a supervisory role, one based perhaps on their previous life and work experience. Others were reluctant to take on that responsibility, feeling a lack of confidence for the supervisory nature of their role as leaders. As worship committee chair, Deirdre knew she had responsibilities in overseeing the work of committee members and worship staff, yet her supervisory role was not clearly spelled out. Bill wanted to make that role more explicit, so that leaders felt more confident about working with others and had more tools for setting and carrying out objectives, dealing with conflict, and using power appropriately.

At the next board meeting, Bill was able to explain more clearly what he meant by supervision. Within this Christian community,

Bill defined supervision as a mentoring relationship between ministry staff and key lay leaders, as well as between key lay leaders and their committee members, within clear guidelines and objectives. He led the board in a discussion of the nature of supervision, both positive and negative, so that assumptions and experiences could be voiced. From this discussion, people realized that "supervisor" was not a role that was to be thrust upon them. Rather, they could shape their supervisory relationships, bringing into play all their best personal qualities.

People grew more excited about the possibility of learning how to offer clearer leadership to others. As conversation flowed, the board members realized that the role of supervisor was not going to be imposed upon them. Each person could offer supervision in distinctly different ways, depending upon his or her unique gifts and personal qualities and depending upon the learning needs of the supervisee and the nature of the tasks before them. As an example, Bill told the board about a previous congregation where he had worked. As senior pastor, he had supervised a staff of five people: two secretaries, one custodian, a church-school director, and an organist/choir director. The secretaries were experienced in their work, showed initiative, and needed little direct supervision. Bill enjoyed weekly meetings that involved mutual feedback, clear communication, and creative exchange of ideas—a supervisory approach that was collegial. On the other hand, the custodian found it hard to organize his work and showed little initiative. Bill needed to supervise daily tasks in a more directive manner, to employ more of a managerial style of supervision. Over the years, Bill had found that supervision is not static; it emerges from the gifts of the individuals involved and the relationship that develops.

For fun, Bill had the board brainstorm qualities that would make a good supervisor at Cross Street United Church. Everyone was surprised by the number of qualities gathered, especially because these were all characteristics they saw in one another:

- willingness to be a leader
- mature faith (prayer life)
- commitment to ministry in the congregation

- experience in congregational and/or denominational life
- knowledge of congregational structure
- gift of listening with empathy
- love of people
- patience with self and others
- ability to hear feelings and thoughts
- wisdom not to take things personally
- clarity about the difference between personal and pastoral issues
- willingness to receive and offer feedback
- facility with conflict management
- knowing when to set clear limits
- awareness of when to support and when to challenge
- sense of humor
- thirst for God's presence in the life and work of the congregation
- desire to look for and think about God's presence

While everyone agreed that not every board member possessed all these qualities, each person had a number of them and a desire to work on other areas. For instance, Flora knew she was a good leader of the United Church Women, able to affirm others and to encourage them to try new projects. She was a good listener but sometimes found herself unable to set clear boundaries around her compassionate listening; sometimes she felt weighed down by others' concerns and was unsure what to do with what she heard. Gus, as chair of the ministry and personnel committee, brought a great deal of supervisory experience from his work in human resources, yet he wanted to explore how his faith might enhance his knowledge of personnel issues. Conflict was an issue on which Deirdre wanted to work; she was nervous about offering constructive feedback, for fear that it might lead to conflict in her role as worship chair. Bill's suggestion to learn more about supervision began to interest the board, and members began to see that they could develop new tools for their leadership roles.

Despite the enthusiasm of the board members, as conversation continued Gus suggested that not everyone is suited to supervise others. Stanley remembered a pompous coach who loved coaching because it allowed him to tell all his old war stories about playing sports. Stanley eventually left the team, because he got tired of listening to the coach and the same old yarns. He realized that the coach was less interested in the team than in meeting his own needs. Deidre talked about a boss in her office whose self-esteem was so fragile that he could lead only by putting others down. She had been relieved when he was moved to another department, because his negative approach undermined the confidence of many employees. Phyllis, a teacher, remembered her days as a student teacher. Time was never set aside for her to reflect on her practice teaching in the classroom, as the teaching supervisor was always busy and having to rush off to one meeting or another. Phyllis was simply seen as cheap help for an overworked teacher, and she was never encouraged in her work. From their experiences, board members could see that they had insights into what qualities would make a poor supervisor as well as what made a good supervisor. From this in-depth discussion, the board agreed to look at ways to address supervision issues in the congregation.

As Bill thought further about supervision in the congregation, he became aware of his main assumption: this work of supervision is a ministry. Personal faith and participation in a faith community form an essential framework for supervision as a ministry. All relationships among Christians, including the supervisory relationship within a congregation, are rooted in a primary relationship with God. God is our rock and our sure foundation, our brother Jesus walks along the road with us, and a restless Spirit beckons us to risk ourselves for others in love. God's grace, abundantly bestowed upon us, supplies us with the grace we are called to offer others. Jesus's ministry of healing and compassion shapes the mutual and empathetic relationships we are called to form. God's Holy Spirit continually fires and inspires our ministry, calling us to responsibility, risk, and challenge, both personally and corporately.

Of course, not all supervision has a faith basis, especially when it is offered in noncongregational settings. However, Bill believed supervision offered in a church setting to be distinctively shaped by faith. Leaders in the church can learn much from business, medicine, and social sciences that will be useful in supervision.

Yet congregational supervision will be marked by faith in a loving and compassionate God, and that faith will reframe learning from other settings.

Some are called to this ministry; some are not. Because this work of supervision is framed and shaped by our primary relationship with God, our supervision is a ministry based upon our call to discipleship. However, although all Christians are called to discipleship, not all are called to this particular ministry. In brainstorming about qualities needed by supervisors, the board was identifying the gifts or charisms of this ministry. Thus, Bill recognized, when he began to work with the board on building supervisory skills, identifying personal gifts for this ministry would be useful and affirming. He would want to be sure that the board and the staff—he would need to think about how to include staff members—spent time on that task in one of the early training sessions.

Supervision as a Learning Relationship

Bill continued to muse about the training course that was taking shape in his head. Over the years, he had developed a conviction that while supervision is a ministry to which only some people are called, the best congregational leader is always open to learning. People who are open to learning do not ignore their knowledge and experience. Rather, they also possess curiosity for what may lie ahead, for the unknown and untried, as well as imagination in combining previous ways of doing things with new possibilities. Openness to learning is also openness to the other person and the gifts that he or she brings to a relationship. Being open to learning creates an attitude of humility, a readiness to be surprised by what lies ahead, and a willingness to learn from others.

For Bill, what kept him excited about supervising a student minister was the opportunity to learn with and from the student at the same time the student was learning with and from him. This learning is not a one-way, hierarchical relationship but one of mutuality. Of course, Bill found great satisfaction in encouraging someone less experienced to try out new liturgies for worship, to work on sermon preparation and delivery, to learn about group dynamics, and to practice pastoral skills by visiting those in need. During an internship a student can learn many skills for leading a congregation, but Bill most enjoyed those times when a student experienced a leap of insight, an "aha!" moment of inspiration when the student felt confirmed in a sense of call, or had clarity about pastoral identity.

Bill also saw himself as a learner in the supervisory relationship, however, and enjoyed conversation prompted by a student's questions—questions that often encouraged him to explore the assumptions he brought to worship, preaching, pastoral care, and Christian education. Many years previously, for example, Bill had worked with an intern, Jake, who was interested in increasing children's participation in all aspects of worship and church governance. Initially, Bill was skeptical of Jake's viewpoint, having been used to children's traditional place in the church school and not in other areas of church life. However, as he and Jake talked about the notion that the church is the whole people of God, not simply the "adults of God," Bill began to see that changes needed to be made in the way he viewed the role of children in the church. With Jake's enthusiasm, Bill engaged the board in a discussion of including children in receiving the sacrament of communion, as well as having young people involved in church committees. Bill appreciated the innovation and challenge of working with interns.

As Bill recalled his year with Jake, he wondered how lay leaders could experience the same sense of mutuality in their supervisory learning relationships. Mutuality requires openness to learning from others, rather than a one-way or top-down approach to supervision. As board members examined issues in supervision, Bill hoped to convey his own openness to learning as he helped board and staff members explore their gifts for ministry leadership and their identity as people of God. He realized that the best way to begin was to look at the concept of learning.

Bill recognized that the approaches to learning are many, but he knew that one model of learning that works well in a supervisory relationship is an action-reflection style. The action consists of various ministry activities. From reflection on those activities, we learn more about ourselves, others, and God's spirit at work. Questions arise, and practices are examined; from those deep reflections on action, we can gain insight for future actions. Reflection follows action, encouraging new action that leads to new reflection, in an ongoing process.

Much learning takes place in an action-reflection pattern, even if unconsciously, and Bill thought the model would probably work well with the board and staff, because some groups in the congregation had already practiced it. He noticed this pattern at worship committee meetings, for example. Each time the members met, they began with a short time for worship to focus on God's presence. Then they reviewed the previous month's services with free-flowing discussion about what had and had not worked. Insights from that discussion influenced what they would plan for upcoming services—a clear process of action-reflection. When Bill had first come to the congregation, this review had been short and always positive. No one wanted to offer any comments that might be construed as criticism. But he had encouraged the committee to take more time for review, looking at both positive and negative experiences. Rather than avoiding those things that had gone badly, Bill believed, the committee could learn much from what had not gone well. Because of Bill's openness to learning and his sense that all experience is a useful basis for learning, people grew braver about expressing their thoughts and suggestions, especially given their desire to encourage and to improve upcoming services. He was certain about this: an action-reflection pattern of learning is beneficial whether one is dealing with student pastors or once-a-month committee meetings. If he used the pattern to help board and staff members learn supervision skills, they would at the same time learn how to use it in their own supervisory work.

Bill recalled another advantage of the action-reflection model he had experienced: it provides a method for ensuring accountability within the supervisory relationship. Each person is accountable to clearly laid-out goals and expectations. Everyone is accountable to others in the faith community and ultimately to God, whether he or she is an intern, a committee chair, or a paid staff person. Bill knew that the youth pastor, Winston, struggled with this concept of accountability with his youth group leaders. He had a relaxed approach and expected that leaders would instinctively know what their roles required. Then he was disappointed when they forgot to show up for meetings or neglected to do the necessary planning for activities. Winston realized that he had not been clear about what he expected of a youth leader. Bill thought Winston could learn both how to support and how to hold accountable the youth leaders within his care.

Bill's excitement about the supervision training was growing. Whether supervising a theological student, youth leaders, committee members, church staff, or small-group ministries, he thought, everyone will benefit from more explicit conversation about the qualities and tools needed in a supervisory relationship.

TWO

LEADERSHIP AND SUPERVISION

The world is a complex place, and its growing complexity is having an impact on congregational life in general and the leadership of congregations in particular. Thomas Hawkins, an educator of congregational leaders and director of off-campus programs at Eastern Illinois University, describes this complexity as he notes significant change in our pace of living. Using leadership consultant Peter Vaill's image of "permanent white water,"[1] Hawkins says we live in a "white water society." Hawkins suggests that "we no longer experience the river of time as a slow, peaceful stream with quiet eddies and calm pools where we have ample opportunity to regain our equilibrium or to recoup our energies." Instead we are "white-water rafting through the rapids of social, technological and demographic change."[2] He talks about shooting down foaming rivers, encountering whirlpools and turbulent, rock-strewn channels. These are powerful images to use in describing ministry and raise a question in my mind as to why anyone would want to be in leadership in such dangerous places. However, with the right craft, finesse in paddling the craft, and the ability to read the river, perhaps leaders of today can embrace the adventure of ministry.

As a canoeist in partnership with a fanatical canoeist, I've learned that with skill, a canoe can be used to navigate both calm and turbulent waters. As a canoeist, you learn how to read the river, examining the surface to discern what's underneath. Sometimes you choose to go with the current; sometimes you go in a completely different direction. You also learn how to use the canoe. A canoe has tremendous maneuvering ability, allowing paddlers to move forward, backward, or sideways; completely turn around; or stay still. Canoes can travel more slowly than the current, buying time, or faster, allowing greater ability to maneuver. As a paddler, you can run a small, shallow rapid and congratulate yourself that you made it with little or no damage. In larger rapids, satisfaction comes from paddling cross-current to get out of the river, looking at the currents to pick a path through the rapids, and using knowledge and skill to thread your way through the obstacles. A path may involve going from one eddy, one pool of quiet water, to another, where you can catch your breath and plan the next move, thus approaching a rapid in small manageable stages, as opposed to flying by the seat of your pants. You cannot outmuscle a river, but if you read the water accurately and use the right technique, the river does the work for you.

In similar fashion, leaders need to be able to read the congregation, getting a sense of what's going on underneath the surface so that they can choose either to go with the flow or to chart another course. They also need skills to navigate conflict without becoming personally embroiled, to find times of solitude even in the midst of chaotic congregational life, to see the bigger picture and not get bogged down in details, yet to attend to details for the smooth running of the church. Fortunately, life in a congregation is not a constant journey through rapids. There are lakes and gentle rivers. At times, the waterway runs out, requiring paddlers to carry or portage equipment to a new waterway. Yet when a section of river runs fast and furious, canoeists can exercise teamwork, flexibility, control, and a variety of techniques and finesse—important qualities for congregational leadership.

Learning to Lead

I observed as a dynamic ordained minister offered a presentation on leadership to a class of theological students, listing qualities he considered essential to a congregational leader: energetic, charismatic, visionary, intuitive, and detail-oriented; as well as a vibrant speaker, a compassionate pastor, a brilliant small-group facilitator, a great motivator, and a person able to engage with all age groups. As the presentation went on and the list of qualities grew longer, I could see student shoulders sag in discouragement. In a debriefing discussion afterward, students confessed to me that they could not live up to the long list of qualities. A great deal has been said and written about leadership and high expectations. Rather than casting a definition of leader into which an individual has to fit, I define leadership more broadly, with the possibility that individuals, lay and ordained, can claim their innate gifts and begin to identify and develop budding gifts. Within a broader definition of leadership, a diversity of leadership gifts and styles necessary for differing needs and contexts can emerge.

Leaders may have any number and types of characteristics. I define leadership within a congregation as *an ability to be in authentic, accountable relationships within a community of faith, using innate and developed gifts for communication, empathy, and encouragement.*

A relationship of authenticity is one in which a person demonstrates congruence between what one believes and how one behaves. No one is perfect, and we don't always live up to the high ideals we profess, yet people of authenticity demonstrate integration of their faith and values with the way they live. A congregation's supervisory role is about encouraging the distinct leadership gifts of those who demonstrate such authenticity.

Along with being authentic, a leader needs to be accountable to a particular committee, a congregation, and ultimately to God. This accountability means that expectations for performance accompany given responsibilities. Typically a minister has a position description that outlines leadership responsibilities and describes to whom he or she is accountable, usually the congregational board. Yet seldom are such expectations outlined for lay leaders in such positions as finance chair, worship chair, church-school teacher, and youth group leader. Defining roles and responsibilities for all leadership positions includes clarifying lines of accountability.

I have identified three areas that are significant for leaders: communication, empathy, and encouragement. Good interpersonal communication is essential for being able to convey ideas, develop relationships, facilitate meetings, and enter into thoughtful conversation. Communication includes the ability to speak and to listen. Accompanying the ability to listen is the particular quality of listening called empathy, the ability to hear and appreciate the feelings of others. Empathy is particularly important in a faith community because we value caring for one another as brothers and sisters in Christ. Empathy is also indicative of self-differentiation and emotional maturity, an ability to see the needs of another person as distinct from our own. Coupled with empathy is the gift of encouraging people in their day-to-day living as well as drawing out emerging and perhaps yet unseen gifts within members of a congregation. I believe I would not be involved so deeply in the church were it not for the gentle nudge of others who saw gifts in me that I had not yet identified. Encouragement includes an ability to move forward with hope in uncertain times. In the complex times in which we live, we are called to live with hope for a kingdom yet to come—a deeply faithful response to God's call. When we encourage members to take on leadership roles and responsibilities—to serve as chair of the board, or financial steward, or pastoral visitor—we need to recognize that we are inviting them to consider their *vocations,* their call from God to serve others. Rather than speaking simply of "helping out" in the congregation, using the term "vocation" puts particular tasks in the realm of our relationship with God and the community of faith.

A supervisory relationship offers a place to talk about leadership qualities, to name and claim innate gifts, and to identify areas for growth. What follows are a few areas to consider as part of that supervisory conversation.

From the Inside Out

Playing with the image of canoeing our way down the rivers of congregational life helps us to understand the need for a leader's personal and interpersonal development. As a canoeist, I have more confidence when faced with turbulent waters if I have developed skill and finesse with my paddling. In facing the turbulent waters of congregational life, I have more confidence when I've worked on my innate skills and continue to develop my leadership abilities. As a supervisor, I'm interested in assisting a supervisee with the same task of building strength and finesse in paddling congregational waters. Disciplined practice can improve strength and finesse. Jim Herrington, pastor, author and conference leader; Robert Creech, pastor; and Trisha Taylor, pastoral counselor, are all involved with Leaders Edge, a nationally recognized leadership-development program. As a writing team, they suggest that developing leadership ability is a process that begins from the inside out. Qualities both inherent and developed in an individual are then demonstrated in outward action. The goal is not perfection, as if that were even possible or desirable. The goal for both supervisor and supervisee is to increase leadership identity and confidence. Herrington and his colleagues name three areas that foster a person's ability to lead: commitment to Christian faith, a loving and encouraging community, and a reflective life.[3]

First, not everyone is able to be articulate about personal faith or theological understanding, yet commitment to Christian faith can be demonstrated in tangible actions such as regular attendance at worship. The chair of a congregational committee who regularly attends worship demonstrates a commitment to God and the faith community through worship, prayer, and praise. I read with interest a denominational resource on the role and function of the core committees of a congregation with primary responsibility for care of the congregation. The writers argued that one of the "most important expectations of members" of these committees "is that each person be involved in a discipline of regular prayer, study, and worship within the congregation to discern the mission of the church."[4] A document outlining the roles and responsibilities of committees names nurture of faith as an important task for leaders. As a supervisor, I encourage a supervisee to engage in a spiritual discipline, perhaps by exploring a variety of disciplines over time such as biblical reading, fasting, and different styles of prayer. Also, in supervisory conversations, we pray together, both to encourage one another in faith, and to learn how to pray. I don't assume that people of faith know how to pray. Often supervisees feel guilty and somewhat fraudulent because they don't have a regular prayer life. I find that praying together breaks through that sense of guilt to deepen faith through prayer.

Second, the support and encouragement of family, friends, and a community of faith fosters budding leadership gifts. In an environment of encouragement, people can face their inner selves, heal the deepest wounds, and deal with life's challenges with hope and courage. To face the truth of our family of origin and its impact on our lives, to address the reality of our behavior, and to accept accountability for our actions, we need a community willing to embrace us in all our humanity. In such a community, grace is offered without judgment but not without accountability. This kind of inner work can be encouraged by a sensitive supervisor within a supervisory relationship of trust. In addition, I inquire about a supervisee's personal community of support: family, friends, and various support groups. Being a leader can be isolating, so I encourage a supervisee to work at developing a network of support.

Third, developing a reflective life offers opportunities to look back over our actions as leader. Through reflecting on our leadership practices, we can become open to and lay the foundation for developing skills that will enhance our ability to lead. For example, we increase our ability to differentiate, to define ourselves and take responsiblity for our behavior while giving space for others to be themselves. As Herrington and his colleagues explain, "Differentiation is the ability to remain connected in relationship to significant people in our lives and yet not have our reactions and behavior determined by them."[5] Differentiation is not an arrival point but a constant process of increasing self-awareness that enables us to stay grounded in our own life purpose without being swayed by the emotional needs of others. Thus, as leaders, we are able to be less anxious, even when others around us are anxious. We can take responsibility for our own emotions without expecting others to become responsible for us. We can become more aware of patterns of thinking that can have a negative and unproductive effect on our leadership. A canoeist needs to be aware of which paddling techniques are working or not working, determining which skills the situation requires, and practicing the less-developed skills to increase personal strength and finesse. Self-awareness and differentiation are particularly useful when turbulent waters are suddenly upon us. Being aware of our anxiety levels and taking time to attend to our personal needs can give us inner muscle or strength to deal with short-term and longer-term crises. Yet we do not do this reflective work alone. Being in a supervisory relationship offers opportunities to share wisdom, encourage one another through listening and prayer, devise strategies for addressing challenging situations, offer feedback, hold each other to account, engage in theological reflection, and accompany each other on the learning journey.

Reading the System

While a canoeist needs certain abilities to navigate, she also needs to step out of the canoe and read the waters up ahead before proceeding. Leaders also need to practice the discipline of stepping out of the stream of our lives to examine what lies ahead and to chart a course. We need to learn how to read the system of a congregation to understand how it works, just as we can learn to read the water surface of a river to understand what is going on underneath. Excellent resources explaining congregation systems are available, making it possible for congregations to offer a leadership-formation course about family and congregation systems.

Leadership is not an isolated venture. It takes place amid a system that has observable rules and ways of behaving. Leadership is a relationship with others in the community. We are interconnected, and our ways of behaving affect each other in conscious and unconscious ways. Two characteristics of any system are degrees of emotional maturity and anxiety. The greater the level of emotional maturity, the better able a system is to deal with anxiety. The reverse is also true: with less emotional maturity, anxiety will escalate. Herrington and friends offer an interesting image to illustrate the relationship between emotional maturity and anxiety levels:

> You might think of the level of emotional maturity as a reservoir, and anxiety as the water level. The larger the reservoir (that is,

the greater the degree of emotional maturity), the more anxiety it can contain without spilling over and producing a problem for the system. The higher the level of water (anxiety), regardless of the size of the reservoir, the closer the system is to overflowing.[6]

For both individuals and systems, anxiety is "our response to threat, whether real or perceived."[7] Our responsibility as leaders is to be aware of our emotional maturity and levels of anxiety in order to offer support to groups and the congregation as a whole. Emotional maturity is demonstrated when we are able to balance personal needs with group needs. Making decisions based solely on group influences without regard for personal needs is a sign of immaturity, as Herrington and others suggest in the following description of the immature leader:

> Emotional reactivity to the group governs every decision; the approval and disapproval of others is the determining factor in all that happens. Feeling liked, accepted, and loved can take precedence over goal-directed activity to the point of allowing the mission of the organization to wither. The leader's hypersensitivity to the demands, wants, needs, desires, and whims of others paralyzes both the leader and the organization.[8]

Autonomy in decision making, to the exclusion of group needs, is another demonstration of immaturity. A leader who is strong, autonomous, and independent may appear to be emotionally mature; however, Herrington et al. suggest otherwise:

> Emotional dependence on others drives the autocratic leader. Others are there to serve the leader's purpose. The compliance of others makes the leader appear successful; the overfunctioning of the leader is matched perfectly by the underfunctioning of his or her constituency. They are looking for a strong leader, rather than thinking for themselves. The autocratic leader is looking for willing followers who allow him or her to think for them.[9]

An opportunity to reflect on leadership style in supervisory conversations deepens awareness of personal needs and the ways these are played out in leadership behaviors. For instance, Paula was newly chairing the Christian education committee. Although talented at creating children's programs, Paula lacked confidence in her leadership ability and reflected on ways to increase her confidence during our supervisory conversations. With her leadership, a number of innovative learning circles for the church school had been designed and implemented. In a follow-up meeting with the Christian education committee, Paula wanted to move on to new projects, while a few committee members wanted to evaluate the learning circles that had just taken place. Paula suggested that the evaluation happen at another meeting, and they moved on to other items on the agenda. Meeting with me for a supervisory conversation, Paula discussed her reluctance to engage in evaluation. For Paula, any feedback on what had taken place would be a negative reflection on what she had planned. Paradoxically, the more confident a person becomes, the more he or she is able to be vulnerable, to be open to feedback, and to admit mistakes. The less confidence a person has, the more she or he will work to cover mistakes and appear always in control even when feeling very much out of control. A supervisor can be a helpful sounding board for feelings as the supervisee works through challenging situations. Paula talked about her need for approval and her fear of criticism. We talked about receiving feedback as a positive process of learning, an opportunity to refine planning for future events. Through support and further reflection, Paula worked at her growing ability to receive and hear feedback not as a personal critique but as an opportunity for learning and leadership formation.

Anxiety is another characteristic of congregational systems, and it comes in two forms: acute and chronic. Acute anxiety arises as a reaction to real threat and is short-term. We deal with the issues, and life returns to normal. Chronic anxiety occurs over a longer period of time, and while it may have been initiated by a particular event, sometimes it develops a life of its own beyond any real threat that may have existed earlier. According to Herrington and colleagues, a chronic state of anxiety "prevents us from functioning at our best and sets us up to escalate additional symptoms of one sort or another." Consequently, "we react rather than respond. We take things personally; we become defensive."[10]

Every system has anxiety, as either a positive or a negative reaction to events. For instance, we may look forward to an upcoming wedding but feel anxious about the planning process. Our ability to deal with anxiety is a measure of our emotional maturity. I believe that one leadership asset is the ability to remain calm in the face of anxiety within the life of a congregation. Nonetheless, many leaders prefer to heighten anxiety in others so as to feel more powerful, more in control, and less anxious themselves in comparison to others. Being aware of such a tendency is essential to individual and communal well-being.

Dealing with anxiety is challenging; it requires thoughtfulness and self-discipline. For example, when an angry person approaches me for conversation, I feel threatened and anxious. Having been in situations like this before, I've had opportunity to reflect on my emotional reactions with my own supervisor, and I have decided that I do not need to react in this way. I am not responsible for the emotions of other people. So I take a deep breath and inwardly step back from the presenting event. I calm myself, listen deeply to what is being said, and hear the issue that is bothering the other person. Although I am being drawn into the conversation, the issue may not be about me at all. And even if the issue is about me, I may have an opportunity to learn something significant from the exchange. Rather than reacting emotionally to this angry person, I can respond thoughtfully and with care.

Lloyd, a faithful member of my congregation, approached me after worship, expressing anger about how I had conducted communion. Faced with Lloyd's anger, I felt a mixture of emotions flooding through me, including reactive anger, embarrassment, and shame. With discipline, I chose not to react to Lloyd but invited him to meet with me to discuss his feelings and concerns further. A few days later, Lloyd was a little calmer, and we had a helpful discussion. Lloyd loved communion and viewed it as a solemn time for deep spiritual union with Jesus Christ. My approach that Sunday had been more energetic, because I included the children in learning about communion as a joyous occasion. Either approach to communion has merit, of course. But as I probed a little deeper, I discovered that Lloyd was dealing with elderly parents who were ill and needed a great deal of his time and energy; he was also working full time and parenting his three teenage children. Lloyd did not need a communion service that seemed chaotic to him in a life that already had too much chaos. He wanted to find a quiet moment to commune with God. Through this pastoral conversation, I was able to see below the surface, address deep pastoral needs, and reflect with Lloyd and the worship committee on how to meet these needs through a variety of worship styles.

While I prefer not to have angry interchanges, I have learned through experience and reflection that every moment is an opportunity for learning. As a supervisor, I invite a supervisee to reflect on events such as these, using the opportunity to review what took place and to see what other strategies might be more useful.

We express our chronic anxiety in community through a variety of behaviors:

1. One way to deal with anxiety is with *conflict*—by provoking a big fight. We want to blame others for what is happening. We insist that our own way is the only right way, often becoming immune to another's point of view. We fixate on the conflict, and even when the conflict resolves, the underlying anxiety remains, waiting to flare up at a moment's notice. We have all met individuals who are perpetually angry and spoiling for a fight.

2. *Distancing* is another way to express anxiety. One person may not speak to another. One group refuses to have anything to do with another group. Individuals or groups leave the church. Sometimes surface issues are addressed and relationships seem to be restored, but if the underlying anxiety is not dealt with, then the same distancing behavior will recur.

3. Another expression of chronic anxiety is *under- and overfunctioning*. This behavior is usually a team effort: one person does not follow through on responsibilities and the other person overcompensates. For instance, a few members of the women's group do all the planning and complain that others don't pull their weight. But those who are not fulfilling their responsibilities don't need to do so, because the others are doing everything. On the other hand, I have been in situations where, even when I am pulling my weight, the anxious overfunctioning colleague does the task again "properly," making it appear that I am underfunctioning. Working in that kind of environment undermines initiative and motivation.

4. A further way of reacting to chronic anxiety is *projecting the system's anxiety* onto one person or group. Sometimes the minister or the head of a fund-raising project that isn't going well becomes the target of this projection. In a chronically anxious congregation, the minister can never preach well enough, visit enough shut-ins, bring in enough new members, or raise enough money. Key lay leaders are always to blame for budget deficits, poor church-school enrollment, and decreases in membership.

Herrington, Creech, and Taylor offer further useful clues that illustrate anxiety bubbling up from below the surface:

- *Reactivity.* When anxiety is below the surface, people react rather than respond, lose ability to listen to others, take comments personally, confuse feelings with opinions, behave with hysteria and/or distance, and lose a sense of playfulness and humor.
- *Herding instinct.* In an anxious system there is intense pressure to conform and no permission to embrace difference or dissent.
- *Blame displacement.* Anxious systems tend to focus on blaming others, taking a victim stance rather than taking responsibility for actions or solutions.
- *Quick Fix.* Rather than working toward a long-term solution, an anxious system goes for the quick fix, even though it fails to address the underlying anxiety.
- *Poor leadership.* An anxious system lacks "a leader who operates with clear vision and thoughtfully held principles." An anxious system needs a leader who can stay connected but maintain difference. "The chronically anxious system is ultimately leaderless" because an anxious system prevents a leader from exercising clear leadership qualities.[11]

A leader needs to be able to see the signs of this anxiety and to avoid being drawn into anxious waters so as to be responsive rather than reactive to congregational anxiety.

Slowing the Pace

To be in touch with our feelings, we need to create a space where we can scan what is going on within us. We need to take time for ourselves. Some people are disciplined enough to set aside a daily time to read Scripture, pray, and listen for God's spirit, a time apart from life for contemplation. To be effective, this time must not be filled with planning, or writing shopping lists, or figuring out what to make for supper. Rather, quiet contemplative time needs to be focused on the relationship between God and self, on what has taken place in the day, and on ways to develop greater awareness and less anxiety. Some people find this sacred space when they are outside walking or jogging. Some have a small prayer center in their home or office with a favorite picture or photograph and a candle to light. Others find that talking with a supervisor, spiritual mentor, close friend, or therapist is useful. I find a morning and evening prayer exercise helpful. The sessions book-end my day, giving me time to anticipate what is coming up, and then to take stock of how the day has gone. I ask myself two questions: "What am I grateful for?" and "What am I not grateful for?"[12] In reflecting on these questions, I am mindful of celebrating positive feelings and events with gratitude. I can also acknowledge and let go of feelings and events for which I not grateful. Areas that need further work can be noted for future discussion with my supervisor or spiritual director or a good friend.

In addition to finding a daily time for prayer and reflection, I need seasonal time. Every spring, my partner and I book a weekend away to walk in the woods and celebrate the movement from winter to spring by noticing wildflowers and budding trees, smelling damp earth, and celebrating the absence of snow. In the fall, we drive into the country to see the fall colors and to prepare ourselves for the oncoming change of season from fall to winter. Taking these seasonal times away from our regular routine broadens our perspective and gets us out of the rut of our patterns of thinking. We become aware of a bigger world beyond immediate daily concerns.

There are other seasons of life: living and dying, celebrations and disappointments. We need to take time to celebrate births and birthdays, a good grade on our child's essay, special moments when everyone is home for a meal at the same time. Celebrating large and small accomplishments is a way of being in touch with our feelings on a regular basis, knowing when we are happy or joyful. In the hurry of life, often these moments go by without being noticed. Conversely, we need to acknowledge our feelings when things do not go well. When our child gets a poor grade, we need to acknowledge our sense of disappointment and own those feelings as ours and not blame the child, who may have a whole set of feelings that he or she wants to experience and express. We need to feel our frustration with a day that did not go well, or the anger that rises when a meeting decision did not go the way we preferred. Denying that we have these feelings will not make them go away. Being aware of these feelings gives us options for how we want to handle them.

A supervisory conversation is another occasion to slow the pace and to take stock of what is going on. In the heat of the moment, I have said and done things that I regret. If I do not tend to my stress, tiredness, anger, and so on, I can be more reactive than responsive, more vengeful than compassionate. Opportunities to reflect with a supervisor give me space to reflect theologically: to revisit a situation, name feelings, think through what happened, and look for meaning in the event by drawing on social analysis, theology, and biblical narrative.[13] The purpose is not simply to rehash the situation but also to reflect honestly in order to learn. When I work with supervisees, I ask, "What have you learned from this situation?" I use this same process in boards and committees as a way to reflect on exasperating situations and to deepen learning. My hope is that this learning can be taken into future situations.

Despite the complexity of today's world, we can navigate our way along life's rivers with finesse. Within a congregation focused on encouraging leadership formation, and with a supportive supervisor, we can discover our innate leadership gifts and further develop blossoming skills in our response to God's call to leadership.

THREE

LEARNING IN CONGREGATIONAL LIFE

Learning is often equated with education, our progress through formal institutional ranks started at an early age and ending—depending on fortitude, economics, and opportunity—with various college degrees. Most educators hope that learning will take place in school, yet there is no guarantee that this will happen. We can teach people—but will they learn? While a great deal of time and energy is expended in formal education, learning does not take place solely in institutional settings. Learning is a process that takes place in various ways throughout our lives, drawing on large and small experiences, shaped by family, friends, and society. Our experiences are integrated into our lives through our attitudes toward events, our ability to reflect on what we encounter, and our capacity to adapt to what lies ahead. For Christians, faith becomes a lens through which to view and interpret our experiences. Our belief in the presence of God in our lives gives us a framework for our reflection and subsequent learning. Thus, I believe that supervision in a faith community needs to include a focus on learning as we sort out our experiences in light of our faith and our call to ministry leadership.

An important aspect of encouraging learning is the heart of the leader, educator, or supervisor. Supervisors must be authentic, fully human. Their words and actions must be congruent. They must be able to admit errors, be respectful of learners in their struggle to learn, and be prepared to be vulnerable. A supervisor is not a superior but one who accompanies as a co-learner. A supervisor is able to name personal gifts and abilities and yet to embody humility and to remain open to learn from the one being supervised. Often supervisors will say something like, "I want to empower the other." However laudable the goal, that understanding still places power with the supervisor. According to respected adult educator Jane Vella, "Teachers do not empower adult learners; they encourage the use of the power that learners were born with."[1] A congregation is a place where mutual empowerment cuts through gender, age, orientation, and culture, and embodies our oneness in Christ.

A faith community is a place where we can respond to God's call to discipleship, particularly through congregational leadership; a place to try out new ways of being, new strategies for relationship, communication skills, constructive conflict management, or whatever life issues we wrestle with. Worship can be an occasion when learning for all ages can be named and celebrated. A congregation can be a supportive and encouraging environment for personal and spiritual exploration. As philosopher Paul Tournier noted, "We can become fully conscious only of what we are able to express to someone else."[2] Through focused conversation with others in our congregation, we can see ourselves anew.

An additional benefit of learning within a faith community is that such a community provides strength when we face issues in society and the world. As individuals, we can feel overwhelmed when we try to take on huge issues in local communities, or in a nation, or across the globe. However, when a community gathers to share learning and wisdom, pooling resources and abilities, huge tasks can be broken down into manageable pieces.

When a congregation member, Don, heard in a sermon about the extent of child poverty in his local community, he felt powerless to do anything to help. Yet as a father of five children, he was moved by the plight of suffering children. He began to talk with congregation members and found that others were just as upset by the statistics. A group formed to talk about the issues, to gather more information, and to brainstorm possible actions. As group members talked, they reflected on their call to feed the hungry and expressed their sense of outrage that children in our society are so vulnerable. By sharing thoughts and feelings, they developed closer relationships with one another and began to feel courage to do more than simply talk about the issue. They considered a number of approaches, from political advocacy to support for a local food bank. However, as they talked further, they decided to work locally. They decided to start a Breakfast Club at a local school to feed children before they began their day of learning. Teachers in the congregation were able to make contacts and set up resources, such as space and cooking facilities. Volunteers signed up to take turns buying supplies, preparing food, and serving the children. Within a few months, children were being fed nutritious food to give them a good start to the day. This Breakfast Club spread to a number of other schools, becoming a project not only of the church but also of community members who were attracted by this tangible outreach to those most vulnerable in our society. Finding such positive ways to learn about and get involved in addressing a social-justice issue within a communal setting brings hope for survival in a complex world.

Lifelong Learning

The term "lifelong learning" reminds me of a comic response to the question, "Have you lived in this village all your life?" to which the elderly farmer replies, "Not yet." No single path toward adulthood and maturity exists, because there is no arrival point. Adulthood is an unfolding process of self-realization that can be stimulated and affirmed in any number of circumstances. Some adults seek further education in a desire not so much to ingest new information as to continue the process of putting old issues to rest, developing self-esteem, and realizing inner potential. In my experience of teaching adult learners, course content is a vehicle for increasing self-awareness, developing deeper relationships with others locally and globally, and realizing gifts and abilities. We can see this concept expressed in such movies as *Educating Rita* and *Shall We Dance?* where the initial desire for learning—through an academic course and a dance class, respectively—is actually an invitation, perhaps by God's Spirit, for deeper personal awareness and reflection on life and relationships.

Learning is not completed upon graduation from high school
or university. Learning is a lifelong process. Even those with little
formal education learn from family, friends, community, life experiences, and their own innate curiosity. I believe it is impossible *not* to
learn. Even those who are resistant to learning learn how to resist.
Yet most people with curiosity enjoy learning, whether through
hobbies, informal courses, travel, reading, Internet surfing, personal crisis, spiritual direction, therapy, raising children, or being
in partnership. Learning encompasses all the ways that we take in
information from life experiences and decide what we will do with
all the new stimuli. Learning can range from the fun of trying new
foods at an ethnic restaurant to the ongoing challenge of dealing
with depression. Learning is very much part of being human.

We need to take learning seriously as an opportunity to discover
more about God, ourselves, and others, especially because a congregation is one of the most distinctive multigenerational gatherings
in society. Adult education in the church tends to be reserved for
Bible study programs, yet in fact learning takes place in all areas of
church life. We learn from preaching, from worship, and from our
interaction with one another on committees. We learn from friendships formed or not formed. We learn about personal integrity
and ethics. We learn how to engage in constructive or destructive
communication and conflict. We learn what community means and
how family systems work. We learn from intentional actions and
decisions and from the lack of actions and decisions.

A faith community can be a wonderful place to learn if we stay
open to the possibility. In applying for a part-time lay leadership
position, I learned about a significant ethical issue. A congregation needed more ministry staff yet was not in a strong financial
position. Several people wanted to step out in faith and hire me, a
young theological student, to do some key work in the church with
children and youth. Several others wanted to spend conservatively
to ensure that the congregation would have no debt at the end of
the year. At a strenuous meeting of the council, members chewed
over the issues, finally deciding to hire me. Within a few hours of
the meeting, I was invited to work for this congregation. Frank, a
longtime member of the church and one of the council members,

took me out for coffee. Frank wanted to let me know that he had spoken strongly against the motion to hire an additional staff person. He did not believe it was fiscally prudent. However, Frank said he believed that God's Spirit was present in the council's discussion and that he would do everything in his power to support and encourage my work. He wanted me to hear his views directly and not through gossip that might skew what he had expressed and what he believed. He did not want me to confuse his opposition to the principle of hiring another person with his delight that I was going to work with the congregation. I was impressed with Frank's integrity. He did not want me to hear from others about his viewpoint, so he was direct and clear. He was able to separate his strongly held position from his respect for the communal decision. And he was true to his word, because his actions fit what he said in his ongoing support for my work. His beliefs and his actions were fully integrated. Frank was one of the most supportive people I experienced in the church, and I continued to learn from his wisdom and from the way he lived his life.

While Frank did not set out to teach me something, I learned a great deal from his behavior. Frank was not intending to "supervise" me, yet his support, his clarity about ethics, and his theological reflection on where God's Spirit was at work in community decisions created a powerful moment of learning for me. Supervision is more than simply overseeing the work of others. While Frank was not my assigned supervisor, our conversation became a serendipitous supervisory conversation because of our theological reflection on events that had taken place at the church council meeting. A supervisory conversation offers an opportunity for reflection on experience to draw forth learning. Supervision can be serendipitous, but I want to encourage a congregation to offer explicit opportunities for regular supervisory conversations, particularly for key lay leaders and staff.

Learning as Formation for Ministry

Learning shapes our beliefs and ways of behaving, derived consciously and unconsciously from cultural and family values, our formal learning, and our life experiences. What we learn in our lives forms us. Formation is a useful word as we think about our spiritual lives. Although used more in Roman Catholic circles, the word "formation" describes the dynamics that form us as people of God. Learning and formation go hand in hand. What we learn forms us, and how we are formed affects how we learn. As faith communities, we need to give more thought to how we learn as people of faith and how our faith is formed as infants, through childhood, adolescence, and adulthood, and into old age.

I often hear congregation leaders referring to members of their congregation as having a "Sunday-school faith," seen as something unformed and childlike. But what does it mean to be an adult? What does it mean to have an adult faith? These are important questions to ask in a congregation that takes formation for adult faith seriously. My hope is that adults will develop a mature faith expressed in actions for social justice and a world transformed for peace. Other leaders may have different goals.

Preparing a learning narrative may create a useful tool for reflecting on what it means to learn, how we have learned in the past, and how we wish to shape our learning in the future. In one small-group setting, Phyllida, a feisty participant, looked back over her life and quipped that there were two kinds of learners: those who learned everything they needed to learn in childhood and simply applied it to the rest of life and those who were continually open to learning with the possibility of transformation. With this insight, she was able to see where she had become stuck in childhood assumptions that she was bringing to current political issues. She began to feel more courageous about stepping out of her comfort zone of previous assumptions to deepen her exploration. "I don't want to get stuck in a rut!" she declared with great energy.

As adults we carry unresolved issues and questions into new relationships and life situations. In addition, we are exposed to personal and societal issues that call into question our previous assumptions. Unresolved issues do not necessarily indicate a lack in our education or upbringing but do offer an opportunity for further learning. Most people believe that once we are adult, we are fully formed, needing no further development or formation. I strongly believe that our formation as adults, as members of society, as disciples of Christ, is a continuous process of lifelong learning.

In my early 20s, having completed my bachelor's degree and having no clear prospects of a job on the horizon, I plunged into a depression. I found a delightful and optimistic woman with whom to talk, a counselor of deep life experience and wisdom. On the surface, my depression related to my discouragement at not finding a job upon completion of my education. However, I discovered layers of personal and family issues bubbling to the surface, issues to which I had not given time and attention over many years of intensive study. Through conversations with my counselor and many hours of reflection and prayer, I began to sort out what I thought and how I felt about my life, relationships with my family and friends, and future directions. I learned so much from this experience of sinking into depression and finding my way out again that it has become a key learning for my life.

As children, we depend on parents and guardians for guidance and are often submissive toward teachers. As adults, we become more independent as we begin to create our own sense of self and determine our own life patterns and goals. Adolescence is often identified as the time when we work toward this autonomy. Young people are often disillusioned to discover that adulthood does not bring ease and clarity in decision making. "I thought adults knew what they were doing!" wailed one young man in a youth group meeting. Adolescents rebel against parents as part of the journey toward adulthood, from a simple acceptance of life and the authority of others to a greater ability to embrace complexity that is part of the adult life journey. Unfortunately, this rebellious period is one of great anxiety, during which the desire to be a child, loved and accepted by parents and other adults, exists in tension with a strong desire to assert a more autonomous presence. Our need to belong, combined with our need to be independent, forms a creative tension that is part of the journey toward adulthood.

Autonomy is an illusion, because we can never be truly independent in the sense of not needing others to fulfill our wants and needs. Yet at the same time, we can't rely totally on others to fulfill them. We continue to be dependent on others for the production of food and clothing, building and transportation, entertainment and information; yet we need to take responsibility for our contribution to society. We are dependent on family members and friends for love and support, on co-workers for affirmation and challenge, while offering love, support, affirmation, and challenge toward others. Perhaps adulthood can be defined as a movement from the simple dependence of childhood to a more complex interdependence as we grow older and more mature. A sign of adulthood may be our ability to manage more complexity in our relationships. Rather than reducing life situations to simple frameworks, an adult is able to balance conflicting ideas and to embrace the ambiguity that is part of human living. The frustration expressed by colleagues who criticize a "Sunday-school faith" is more a response to others' simple dependence on uncomplicated ideas. A congregation is a place where we can be invited to reflect on what it means to be an adult and to have an adult faith, a place where our learning narrative can be brought to consciousness.

Transformative Learning

Adult educator Patricia Cranton suggests that transformative learning "occurs when, through critical self-reflection, an individual revises old or develops new assumptions, beliefs, or ways of seeing the world."[3] I believe that all learning is transformative. God calls us to be transformed, to adopt life-affirming rather than death-dealing ways of living. God desires our transformation from people who lack self-worth to people who recognize our worth as God's beloved. We are called from individualistic to communal ways of being, from serving self to serving others, from despair to hope, and so on. Learning in a congregation has the potential to stimulate and support transformation, and the supervisory conversation can be an occasion to focus on learning. Both the supervisor and supervisee need to develop learning goals as part of a learning covenant. More will be said about how to develop learning goals within a learning covenant in chapter 6. While learning goals are not meant to limit learning that might arise serendipitously, a goal does offer a framework for critical reflection that may lead toward transformation.

In exploring the notion of transformative learning, Cranton identifies three strands: subject-oriented, consumer-oriented, and emancipatory learning. These categories are not mutually exclusive but nonetheless give us language to talk about learning. *Subject-oriented learning* is "the acquisition of content, whether that is facts, concepts, problem-solving strategies, or technical or practical skills."[4] Learning content through methods such as rote memorization comes in and out of fashion yet must not be ignored. Learning passages from the Bible by rote was one teaching technique much heralded in the past; it is still a foundational teaching tool in more evangelical circles where "sword drills" encourage memorization of Scripture passages. While accessing Scripture out of context and without interpretation is not necessarily helpful to transformative learning, not knowing any biblical texts at all is even less helpful. In supervision, I encourage supervisees to read the lectionary passages each week as a way to familiarize themselves with Scripture texts. Often the texts resonate with experiences that took place within the week, thus providing a lens through which to view and reflect upon events, a useful way to encourage theological reflection.

In *consumer-oriented learning,* individuals identify what they wish to learn and seek the resources to fulfill their learning needs, perhaps even by looking for a content-oriented course. The distinction is that in "subject-oriented learning, learners turn the decision making over to the expert; in consumer-oriented learning, learners make each decision."[5] With a consumer orientation, learners are highly motivated, usually setting their own objectives, finding resources, and evaluating their progress in meeting their goals. The learning will be relevant and of great interest to the learner. As people become more oriented toward computers and Web surfing, adults are discovering worlds of learning accessible at their fingertips. In supervising members of a worship committee, I encouraged them to set a learning goal for the year. Newer members wanted to learn more about worship resources. Greatly motivated by their learning goal, they used the Internet to research denominational Web sites that offered creative materials for everything from unpacking biblical texts for sermon preparation to offering stimulating children's stories, from youth-focused biblical dramas to bulletin clip-art, from liturgies for special events like affirming the covenant of marriage to lists of suggested hymns and anthems for each Sunday. They thoroughly enjoyed investigating resources available to them in their role as worship leaders.

Cranton's third category, *emancipatory learning,* has a more revolutionary quality and is defined as "a process of freeing ourselves from forces that limit our options and our control over our lives, forces that have been taken for granted or seen as beyond our control."[6] People who are illiterate experience emancipatory learning when they learn how to read and find the world opened up in previously unimagined ways. Emancipatory learning invites "an individual to engage in informal or formal learning and to reflect on basic assumptions and beliefs"[7] in order to be released from previous oppression by people, systems, and ideas that have been controlling and disempowering. In a pastoral conversation Wanda revealed to me long-term physical abuse by her husband. I knew from experience that the journey toward emancipation from the oppression of abuse is long and arduous. I asked her if she and I could set up a supervisory group for reflection on her situation, to offer support as she gathered information, decided future directions, and began the work of healing. She agreed that a support network would be a positive first step, because she was feeling a great sense of isolation. She identified three women whom she could trust with her story. After speaking individually with each woman about the request to form a supervisory group, we had a first meeting. These women brought gifts of clarity and compassion as they listened to Wanda's story. However, from their life experience they knew that challenges lay ahead. Because of the upheaval in assumptions and worldview inherent in emancipatory learning, this process is often painful and challenging. In my pastoral experience the closer an individual comes to seeing a contradiction between what was previously believed and the possibility of new directions, the more resistance she or he will express. According to Cranton:

If learners overcome the initial personal and social resistance to questioning their assumptions and beliefs and become engaged in critical self-reflection, emancipatory learning does not become any less disquieting. A learner questioning personal psychological beliefs or assumptions related to his or her social context can experience considerable emotional upheaval.[8]

This supervisory group offered Wanda the support she needed to look at her life and to choose more positive directions. In subsequent meetings, group members encouraged her to set goals for herself and checked in with her regularly to support the new steps she was taking. With the encouragement of three strong women, Wanda began to imagine and live a different life for herself.

Encouraging Transformative Learning

Transformative learning emerges from an assumption that there are no absolute truths or universal ways of constructing reality. Instead, we are invited to reflect on our perceptions of the world while opening ourselves to the possibility of change. Cranton suggests:

We interpret our experiences and the things we encounter in our own way; what we make of the world is a result of our perceptions of our experiences. Transformative learning, then, is a process of examining, questioning, validating, and revising these perceptions.[9]

A congregation can be a place to encourage transformative learning through critical reflection on our experiences. For this experience to be most effective, learners need:

- access to accurate and complete information
- freedom from coercion
- a safe place for self-determination
- ability to weigh evidence and assess differing positions openly

- openness to alternate approaches and ways of thinking
- ability to reflect critically
- shared opportunities to question, challenge, and listen

To engage in transformative learning, the learner needs to reflect on current beliefs and thoughts to choose new ways of believing and thinking. Reflection is an important tool in transformative learning. Cranton suggests three strands of reflection: content, process, and premise. *Content reflection* is an exploration of the content of a problem. If a car breaks down, a mechanic examines the engine to figure out what is going on. In *process reflection,* rather than being focused on the engine, the mechanic thinks about the best way to solve the problem. For instance, a mechanic may reflect on what resources will be helpful, what experts or manuals need to be consulted, what kinds of tools will be useful for fixing the engine. A further layer of reflection, *premise reflection,* takes another step back in questioning the problem itself. A mechanic may ask: Why am I fixing this car? Is it worth fixing? Do I really need a new engine or a brand-new car?

When Wanda, discussed above, sought to make positive changes in her life, she used content, process, and premise reflection as she engaged in transformative learning. Initially, Wanda needed to identify the problem that needed to be fixed. If she was going to fix this problem, Wanda had to figure out what resources were available to her, such as legal aid, a women's shelter, and a support group. In taking a new direction in her life, Wanda asked tough premise questions exploring whether to stay in the marital relationship or leave. Instead of blaming herself and staying in a potentially life-threatening situation, Wanda realized that she needed to take new directions.

In supervising a newly formed group of lay readers, we moved through content, process, and premise reflection as preparation for reading Scripture. The learning goal for the group was to read Scripture lessons during worship. Content reflection drew the lay readers to look at texts; it focused on how to pronounce words, how to speak clearly, and how to use a microphone. Adding a layer of process reflection, we looked at lectionary resources, commentaries that gave background information about the text, and a reading style that would convey the meaning of what they were saying. Premise reflection took us to a discussion of why they were reading Scripture, the meaning of being lay leaders in a congregation that encouraged lay leadership in worship, and the meaning of speaking God's word to the congregation. From an initial willingness to read Scripture in worship services, the group members were transformed into accomplished readers with a vocational sense of the importance of imparting God's word each Sunday.

Reflection is not a straightforward process that leads through linear steps. Along with the possibility that a learner may reject new data, ideas, or beliefs, Cranton observes that reflection includes "curiosity, confusion, testing, withdrawal, exploration and reflection, turning to others, renewed interest and excitement, reorientation, equilibrium, and advocacy."[10] Also, as much as leaders may want a community of faith to go in particular directions or to learn new concepts, transformative learning cannot be forced from the outside. "Learners must decide to undergo the process; otherwise educators indoctrinate and coerce rather than educate."[11] Transformative learning can be strenuous work; therefore, a learner needs a stable self-concept to have the strength to engage in critical reflection and new learning. However, once a willingness to learn is evident, a leader, educator, or supervisor can stimulate learning through various tools for critical reflection, such as:

Role playing:
- Reverse roles normally played.
- Take the part of a person you have studied.
- Write a biography of someone else.
- Express opinions opposite to your own.

Simulating and game-playing:
- Lay out a situation where decisions need to be made.
- Simulate a group of elderly people with various losses.
- Reflect on your own life as a teenager to imagine the stress for present-day teens.
- Act out life situations.

Writing a life history or learning narrative:
- Create a learning narrative as outlined in the topic and tool found on ensuing pages.
- Write or express artistically a spiritual journey.

Journal writing:
- Keep a two-column journal, one side for what happened and the other for thoughts, feelings, related experiences, or images.
- Write secular or sacred poetry.
- Write to a person; write as someone else.
- Keep a dialogue journal with responses from someone else.

Experiential learning:
- Set aside time for critical discourse before, during, and after the experience.
- Develop questions for reflection with the group.
- Examine the difference between theory and the experience and compare with related experiences.
- Discuss how to give, receive, and act on feedback.
- Brainstorm feelings, thoughts, and insights.

Critical incidents:
- Role-play a critical incident.
- Share incidents in pairs or group.
- Reflect in small groups and large groups.
- Plan for future actions. What would you do differently? What will you do next time?
- Ensure that all residual negative or strong feelings have been addressed.

Theological reflection:
- Use tools for theological reflection to make a connection between life events and faith, between our story and the biblical story.
- Be aware of reflection that moves from content to process to premise.

Learning can be a strenuous yet rewarding process, and a congregation can be a safe and encouraging environment for transformative learning. The following learning narrative method may be a useful tool to invite adult learners to become open life-long learners.

Learning Narrative

Learning takes place in all aspects of our lives, but often we confine learning to formal institutional educational settings. A supervisory relationship offers a place to explore intentionally how and in what ways we have learned. As an avid adult educator, Pierre Domincé developed a method to encourage adult learners to reflect on how they have learned throughout their lives.[12] He uses his method in a university setting to acquaint students with the way "they learn through the vehicles of informal education and experiential learning."[13] I have adapted his method for use in small-group settings as a process of developing a learning narrative, a story of our life learning. This process can be used as a short-term study in ongoing groups, or in groups formed specifically to engage in this reflection as part of a program of developing leadership gifts, or as an individual reflection in a supervisory conversation.

A learning narrative is one method to help adults look at their entire lives as a locus for learning. In church life, we use the language of storytelling. We listen to the stories of the Old and New Testaments and attempt to connect the biblical story with the stories of our lives. Some of the benefits of creating and telling the story of our learning include:

- Becoming aware of how interconnected we are.
- Understanding connections between our personal story and societal movements.
- Appreciating the different ways we each learn and organize our lives.
- Valuing each life as unique.

None of us lives in isolation. We are shaped by many people and events. Self-awareness is raised when we become more conscious of the intricate web of living. Domincé suggests that learning narratives

> can help adult learners recognize social and interpersonal influ-
> ences on their lives and educational activities. Preparing a life
> history focused on learning can also clarify the interdependence
> of biographical themes, major life transitions, and educational
> activities, calling learners' attention to both processes and out-
> comes in their lives and learning. . . . These narratives can also
> reveal formerly hidden influences, such as cultural traditions
> and beliefs.[14]

Through greater awareness we may appreciate aspects of our lives previously unexplored. I have used the learning narrative approach in pastoral visiting by modifying the questions to encourage people to talk about and reflect on their life stories to discover the learning embedded within. I recall a pastoral conversation with Vera, a member of my first parish. To look at Vera, you would simply see a frail, elderly woman, and Vera was feeling vulnerable and fragile at this point in her life. In listening to responses to questions about her life, I discovered that she had lived through World War II in Europe and had raised three children as a war widow. She described hard times, yet as she looked back on her experiences, she realized that she was proud of the strength and determination that had brought her through many crises and the spirit of those in her community who had cared for one another by sharing the little they had. She remembered those times as experiences that had formed her identity and her values, and learned again that although her body was frail, she had the same spirit and determination to face what lay ahead.

Not all memories have such a glow to them. One war veteran I visited recalled his naivete in signing up as a very young man to "fight the good fight" and discovering that the people he was being trained to kill were just as young and vulnerable as he was. He began to question the assumptions of going to war and "fighting Hitler." In looking back over his life, he became aware that his war experiences had been a pivotal moment of learning when he matured as an adult; although realizing that the war needed to be fought, he shifted from innocently assuming the values of his family and peers to more deeply appreciating the complexity of world politics. In these two examples, we can see that by looking back over our lives we can identify moments from which we learn and can continue to learn. A learning narrative offers a tool to learn about how we learn, when we have learned, and what we have learned, to shed light on what has shaped our beliefs and ways of being. Whether working with a small group, engaging in a pastoral conversation, or reflecting in a supervisory conversation, understanding how and what we learn can encourage openness to learning from our lives.

Learning Narrative

A learning narrative is one way to explore not only how we learn but also the key moments when we have learned something that seems significant. Much of our education occurs in formal institutional settings. However, learning takes place throughout our lives in myriad forms. We can develop a learning narrative both individually and with others. A facilitator or supervisor can use the following outline:

Step 1: Introduction

A first meeting can be a time of sharing food, getting to know one another, and introducing the notion of a learning narrative. Distribute the questions outlined below as a guide for reflecting on learning in general. The questions are designed to stimulate reflection on significant learning moments. In subsequent sessions, participants can take turns offering oral responses to the questions, and then deepen the experience through written work as described below.

Step 2: Oral Narratives

Participants will reflect on the questions below individually; then, with a supervisor or in a small group, participants will share aloud what insights arose from that reflection. Participants may find it helpful to make notes in the reflection time to assist memory. As facilitator, you may choose to offer your presentation first, unless someone else is eager to begin. Give each person 20 to 30 minutes to present, with an additional 10 minutes for clarifying questions and constructive comments from the group. As many as three people might present at each gathering. Or the whole group can share thoughts about one chosen question.

Learning Narrative Questions

Use the following list as a guideline for your oral and written narratives. Do not be restricted by these questions. Rather, use them as a jumping-off point to dive into the pool of your narrative.

- Education is . . . ? Learning is . . . ?
- What is the learning history of my family (education, attitudes toward education, learning aptitudes, etc.)? What attitude toward education has been passed on to me?
- What is my learning history? (Formal: public school, high school, university. Informal: family, friends, work, community, church.)
- What is my attitude toward formal and informal learning?
- What kind of experience did I have at school?
- What do I believe about myself as a learner? What has shaped this belief? What do I want to change?
- How have family life, formal schooling, and life events influenced my attitude toward learning?
- What have been several transformational moments in my life? Describe the impact of several traumas. What learning arose from these experiences?
- What kind of learning attracts me most? What learning is challenging?
- What image or metaphor describes my self-identity as learner?
- Am I a confident learner? Or am I afraid of learning?

- What excites me as I anticipate new learning opportunities? What challenges do I anticipate? What gaps in my learning do I want to address?

Step 3: Written Narratives

After sharing aloud with the group or with your supervisor, take time to reflect further by writing a reflection on your learning narrative. The following questions may assist your writing: What surprised you? Where were you challenged? What discoveries did you make? What do you want to explore further?

Step 4: Presenting Written Narratives

In a subsequent meeting, share written narratives with one another. Engage in discussion about each person's presentation to draw out central themes and affirm the ongoing learning journey.

The Learning Environment

A congregation can be a place where people reflect on their lives, a process requiring openness and vulnerability. To create an environment that encourages an adult learner, Vella suggests 12 principles that honor the learner as adult and incorporate insights from quantum thinking. These 12 principles are a useful framework for the supervisory relationship.

1. Needs Assessment. Adult learners need to participate in their own learning by naming their needs and expectations. At the beginning of a supervisory relationship, discussing what the supervisee and supervisor wish to learn helps to clarify who the learners are and what expectations they bring to the learning.

2. Safety. Learning takes place best in a safe environment, and with safe content and process. On the other hand, Vella observes that "Safety does not obviate the natural challenge of learning new concepts, skills, or attitudes. Safety does not take away any of the hard work involved in learning."[15] Creating a safe environment increases the ability of learners to address challenging concepts. Safety is fortified when learners trust in the competence of the supervisor and the structure of the learning, and trust in the relevance of the learning objectives. By involving learners in expressing their learning needs, experiences, and opinions about the learning task, trust is built. Also, creating a nonjudgmental environment by affirming each learner for his or her contributions shares power among learners. Finally, learning deepens when it moves from simple to complex. The lay readers' group mentioned above began with simpler tasks such as reading Scripture texts aloud and practicing with the lectern microphone. The group then moved to more complex tasks of researching the texts and finally of reflecting on the meaning of reading Scripture during worship.

3. Sound Relationships. Learning is enhanced when attention is paid to the relationship between supervisor and supervisee. Development of this relationship needs to include awareness of power and how it is used, as well as respect for one another. In Vella's experience, "Sound relationships for learning involve respect, safety, open communication, listening, and humility."[16]

4. Sequence of Content and Reinforcement. Learning takes conscious effort that can be assisted by care in planning the sequence of content. As mentioned above, movement from simple to complex affirms the learner as he or she moves through layers of learning. Also, a learner's confidence can be increased in a movement from being supported in initial efforts to flying solo.

Vernon, chair of finance, wanted to begin each committee meeting with prayer, but he felt completely out of his depth in this area. With prayer at meetings as his goal, he asked me to write a few prayers that he could use. I asked him to expand his goal to include writing his own prayers, and I suggested that we could work on this together. We began by looking at a few prayers in some resources, and then discussing what was being said in these prayers. We discussed Vernon's prayer life and ways that he could express his faith through writing his own prayers to begin the meetings. He wrote a few sample prayers that we refined. Vernon moved from writing somewhat stilted formal prayers to writing prayers in his natural voice, expressing his own faith. After increasing his confidence in writing and offering prayers at meetings, Vernon moved to offering a prayer spontaneously at a gathering—flying solo. Learning is also reinforced by engaging the content in different ways until the learning is accomplished.

5. Praxis. Action-reflection learning is more than simply putting theory into practice; it is about *praxis,* reflecting on activities and discovering the theory embedded. Praxis brings questions arising from practice to theoretical understanding, so that action challenges theory, which in turn stimulates action, in an ongoing spiral.

Vernon moved from the rote practice of saying a prayer at the beginning of a finance meeting to reflecting on his faith and on why prayer was an important component of the meeting for him. As he began to write prayers, he thought about what he believed and the purpose of prayer, in a desire to express his faith and not simply go through the motions of praying. His reflective process continued as he prayed and reflected on prayer; it brought new depth to his public prayers as well as his personal faith.

6. Respect. Learners can and must be decision makers in their learning. Vella strongly advises supervisors, "Don't ever do what the learner can do; don't ever decide what the learner can decide."[17]

7. Ideas, Feelings, and Actions. As supervisors, we need to encourage all kinds of approaches to learning that will draw out ideas, feelings, and actions. For instance, theological reflection can be done in written form, but it can also include painting, poetry, dance, and group dialogue.

8. Immediacy. Learning needs to be immediately useful and accessible.

9. Clear Roles and Role Development. The role of the supervisor is co-learner. Although the supervisor may begin with more knowledge, the supervisory relationship needs to ensure that the supervisee gains more esteem and power in the learning process. Vella reflected on a conversation she had with Paulo Freire, an adult educator who framed a liberationist approach to learning. While a supervisee may initially be somewhat dependent on the supervisor, that position will shift as the supervisee gains more confidence.

Freire observed that "Only the student can name the moment of the death of the professor."[18]

10. Teamwork. Using small groups in the learning process engages learning in relationship, the challenge of other learners, and experiences of peer review and feedback.

11. Engagement. Learners are not passive recipients; they need to be fully engaged in the learning. Linked to praxis, engagement means to learn "actively in [addressing] strategic issues of their organizations and of the community"[19] and particularly in doing tasks that have meaning. Simply doing busywork is not effective in learning.

12. Accountability. Both the supervisor and supervisee need to assess what has been learned by asking such questions as: Did we learn what we set out to learn? What has changed? What insights have been gained? Supervisor and supervisee are accountable to themselves as individuals, to one another, and to the congregation.

Vella's principles offer a useful framework for those developing a supervisory relationship with adult learners. In addition, Wilma Fraser, another respected expert and writer on adult continuing education, suggests additional principles to keep in mind in transformative learning.

1. In encouraging experiential learning, we need to acknowledge our multilayered selves: body, mind, emotions, thoughts, imagination, analysis, and so on.
2. Learning takes place best in a supportive environment, and in particular, group process allows for checking out our perceptions socially with input from others.
3. As we examine our experiences, we need to be aware of the societal and familial influences embedded in our ways of thinking and ways of being.
4. We need to incorporate a power analysis in our reflection on our experiences.
5. Emerging feelings need to be incorporated as part of the reflection on learning, not dismissed or challenged or seen as extraneous to the learning process. Fraser

reminds us that "New experiences will emerge as a result of the conflict between old assumptions and fresh understandings. This [conflict] will generate a range of emotions, including anger and fear."[20]

Acknowledging the multilayered adult person and respecting adults' needs as learners are essential in encouraging lifelong learners in a congregation, as well as in developing an open and trusting supervisory relationship.

Learning is a complex process, and congregations can be places where safe learning is encouraged. Whether in a one-on-one supervisory relationship or in small groups, we can deliberately offer opportunities to reflect on how we learn and on what learning has taken place in our lives, so that we may open ourselves to future transformative learning with courage and hope.

FOUR

CONFLICT AND SUPERVISION

Dealing with conflict is one of the most challenging areas of church life, partly because most people would rather believe that Christians don't fight and partly because few have learned how to engage in conflict well. In a compilation of articles on conflict, Roy Pneuman, a former senior consultant with the Alban Institute who writes about team building and conflict management, comments:

> Conflict is inevitable. Conflict is part of every relationship in life, and it is inherently neither good nor evil. Conflict creates the energy that makes change possible. Conflict becomes destructive when we mismanage it. Well-managed conflict is usually not even recognized or labeled as conflict, yet we feel exhilarated when we manage our differences in such a way that each party comes away feeling good.[1]

Because conflict is inevitable and part of every relationship, learning about the nature of conflict and how to fight fair is an important life skill. Learning how to manage conflict may lessen the escalation that can occur and ease the fear and anxiety that attend discord. Conflict management will be part of supervisory conversations, because differences will arise in congregational life and leadership. Also, conflict may occur between supervisor and supervisee, so taking time to discuss the nature of conflict as well as a process for addressing disagreements will be helpful.

Useful resources on the topic of church conflict are abundant as a result of the extent of mismanaged conflict evident in the church. Rather than exploring the vast topic of conflict, this chapter will focus on conflict as it applies to the supervisory relationship. While we have high hopes that all relationships will be amicable, we need to be realistic: conflict is part of all human interactions. Conflict is even more likely in supervision, because of the power differential and because of the emphasis on feedback and evaluation—two aspects that increase the possibility of tension.

If we believe that Christians do not fight or perhaps should not engage in conflict, then we might turn to Matthew and find a scripture passage demonstrating that not only did the early church struggle with difference; in addition, the members had a process for dealing with conflict:

> If another member of the church sins against you, go and point out the fault when the two of you are alone. If the member listens to you, you have regained that one. But if you are not listened to, take one or two others along with you so that every word may be confirmed by the evidence of two or three witnesses. If the member refuses to listen to them, tell it to the church; and if the offender refuses to listen even to the church, let such a one be to you as a Gentile and a tax collector.
>
> Matthew 8:15–17

What this text describes is a series of conversations intended to resolve conflict. First, when an initial conflict arises, speak directly with the other person. Deirdre, chair of worship, disliked confrontation in any form, yet she found that most disagreements were quickly resolved through direct conversation. That was her experience in supervising Angus, a member of the flower committee. Angus kept forgetting to dispose of the flowers after the worship service. Deirdre became frustrated at finding dying flowers in the sanctuary later in the week. However, instead of stewing about this issue, Deirdre decided to ask gently if she could help Angus in clearing up the flowers. Deirdre discovered that Angus had to pick up his four children from church school immediately after the worship service and deliver them to various Sunday-afternoon activities. Despite good intentions, Angus simply forgot about the flowers in his flurry to gather children and leave the church. After some discussion, Deirdre and Angus decided that if Angus could arrange for the flowers to be delivered and displayed for worship, one of the youth members could distribute the flowers to older members of the congregation after the service. They easily identified a young person who was eager to take on this job.

Most conflicts can be resolved quickly with direct conversation. However, if such quick resolution is not possible, then a second layer of conversation is useful. Deirdre found this additional layer helpful in an ongoing conversation with the church organist, Yun Sung. Week after week, Yun Sung arrived late on Sunday morning. Once she had dashed into church, the choir needed to warm up, rehearse, and get ready for the processional hymn. On several Sundays the worship service was late in starting because the choir was not ready. Starting the service late frustrated other worship leaders, as well as the church-school teachers. Deirdre found a quiet moment during the week to speak with Yun Sung about this problem. Yun Sung immediately became defensive and refused to talk further about the issue. When the problem persisted, Deirdre sought wisdom from the congregation's ministry and personnel committee. The committee chair, Gus, decided to invite Yun Sung out for lunch along with Deirdre.

Evidently, Deirdre's concern was one of a number of issues that had arisen over a period of months. Gus had expertise in personnel issues and liked to begin with friendly conversation before moving on to more sensitive matters. In Gus's experience, personnel issues often masked personal problems such as illness or stress at home that could often be addressed in a compassionate, pastoral conversation. As it turned out, the lunch conversation with Yun Sung was an opportunity to resolve several issues, amicably restoring peace on Sunday mornings. However, such resolution is not always possible.

A few years previously, Gus had had to deal with a youth pastor, Jonah, whose erratic and immature behavior was a concern to parents of youth. After numerous attempts at friendly conversation, Gus had to "tell it to the church" by recommending to the board that Jonah be put under a performance-evaluation process to address the behavior. When a hoped-for change in performance did not materialize, resolution became impossible, and eventually the youth pastor had to be dismissed. Although Gus did not want Jonah to be as "a Gentile and a tax collector" to him, he did have a responsibility to terminate Jonah's contract. Gus followed a careful process for dismissal, using guidelines set out by the denomination. He knew from his work experience that lawsuits for wrongful dismissal are a possibility, even in the church, if an organization does not follow clear and fair dismissal policies. Ensuring that such policies are in place is essential in a congregation. No one wants to deal with dismissing staff, yet having clear policies eases the stress at such difficult times.

Dismissal of a staff person is painful, yet at times necessary. What can be more difficult is dismissing a paid or volunteer congregation member from a leadership position? An experienced pastor, Denise Goodman observes that "churches are vulnerable to conflict because they lack the ability to impose sanctions which, in healthy families and workplaces, enforce some form of accountability."[2] Some faith communities, such as the Amish, have clear sanctions that govern members. In most congregations, however, "sanctions often are unspoken and underground."[3] Congregation members tend to put up with bad behavior rather than confront it. One congregation's struggle with Sandy offers a case in point.

Sandy had grown up in the community and had attended Cross Street United Church since she was a small child. She had always been referred to as eccentric, but as she aged, her eccentricity became more pronounced, as demonstrated in angry outbursts and rants about issues that had no foundation. She loved working with very young children in the kindergarten program of church school and seemed at her best in that context. Since church-school policy required teachers to work in teams, Sandy's behavior was tempered by the other team member. However, after two episodes in which she exploded with anger at a young child, the church-school committee decided that Sandy was not an appropriate person to work with those who were so vulnerable. The group approached the ministry and personnel committee for assistance.

A member of that committee and two members who had known Sandy for many years met with her to explain that her conduct was not appropriate—especially not when working with young children. Because a church is a public gathering, Sandy was welcome to continue attending Cross Street United Church; however, she was told that her angry outbursts would not be tolerated. Sandy was angry at being denied time with the children and tried several times to head downstairs to church school, yet Gus offered firm yet compassionate reminders that although she was welcome at worship, she could not be involved with the church school. This difficult experience at Cross Street United gave the ministry and personnel committee an opportunity to discuss a number of issues. The group was able to develop policies useful in other situations with difficult members, as well as policies and procedures regarding risk assessment with children and vulnerable adults—material that can be found in chapter 5. Although most people prefer to avoid conflict at all costs and generally view conflict as a negative aspect of relationships, not all conflict is bad, and often important learning can come from even the most difficult situations.

Characteristics of Conflict

As mentioned above, conflict is a normal part of all human relationships. Speed B. Leas, who consults with religious organizations on conflict resolution, warns that conflict is difficult not only "because one rarely knows how others (especially groups) will respond to any given situation," but also because there are no quick-fix solutions to conflict.[4] As Christians, we are called to love our neighbor as ourselves and to care for others in need, an obligation that includes working on our relationships with each other and working through conflict. In a congregation people can develop healthy approaches to expressing conflict and can learn to name and practice appropriate behavior both within the congregation and elsewhere in their lives. Supervisory conversations can include exploration of healthy approaches to conflict, thus encouraging new patterns for dealing with difference of opinions and values so that supervisor and supervisee feel better equipped with information and insights about conflict.

Conflict can range from gentle difference of opinion all the way to full-blown warfare. Leas identifies five levels of conflict, beginning with disagreement. In this initial level people are involved in cooperative problem-solving; both are committed to finding a solution, using language that is clear and specific to the problem at hand. As conflict escalates to a second level, people move from problem solving to self-protection, defending their own needs and outcomes. Rather than using language that encourages mutual solutions, they use less specific language to describe their disagreement. One general phrase I hear used in conflict situations is, "People are saying that . . . ," a phrase meant to imply that other people are unhappy with the situation in addition to the person in front of me. In third-level conflict, people's goals move from self-protection to a desire to win. At this point, speech takes on an "us-versus-them" quality, and perceptions become facts. As conflict escalates in level four, winning can happen only when radical change takes place, such as the removal of people from their positions. And finally, at level five, winning takes on a fanaticism, as people "feel themselves called by God to eradicate from the earth those to whom they are opposed."[5]

Despite the possibility for escalation of conflict, within most relationships conflict is potentially healthy. Differences of opinion, approach, and feelings are inevitable in relationships and groups where diversity is respected and valued. Exploring differences can enrich a relationship or community by broadening perspectives on issues and enlarging interests. An opportunity for open expression of fears evoked by conflict has the potential for bringing greater intimacy in a relationship and for increasing trust.

One layer of awareness about conflict is in our attitude toward it, either positive or negative. When people are asked, "What's the first thing that comes to mind when you hear the word 'conflict'?" responses are usually negative and involve words like anxiety, tension, shouting, and discomfort. Conflict can be negative when it undermines morale or reinforces poor self-worth. But it can be positive when people have an opportunity to put issues on the table in an open discussion. Airing differences and understanding one another better are positive outcomes of conflict. Conflict can be negative when it diverts energy from normal activities and issues and becomes a central focus of congregational life. When language devolves into name-calling and "them's fightin' words," then authentic communication becomes impossible. From a positive perspective, conflict can serve to release pent-up feelings and stress if managed through constructive communication and behavior. Although facing someone who disagrees with me can be stressful, we can find satisfaction in working through problems, celebrating a resolution of tension, and learning more about each other. Working through conflict can be a path to greater intimacy.

Encountering ideas different from our own can challenge our assumptions and attitudes and offer an opportunity for learning and growth. When confronted with a different way of doing or thinking about things, we have an opportunity to review how and why we do what we do. To explore conflict, we need to establish ways to communicate differences in a respectful manner, beginning with an appreciation of others' points of view and an openness to the possibility of change rather than an insistence that there is only one right way of being or operating. Listening to differing experiences gives us insight into how others feel and think. Conflict can be negative, but it also contains the seeds of greater understanding, intimacy, and compassion.

Awareness of Conflict

Supervision can help us become more aware of how we react to conflict. In a supervisory relationship I like to invite conversation about what we feel and think about conflict, how our families dealt with disagreement, and what conflict-management style we prefer. When good rapport has built up, a supervisory relationship offers an environment in which we can explore issues that surround conflict, such as the way power is used and abused, as well as personal issues that might frame approaches to conflict. Working on differences of opinion and taking varied approaches to tasks offer us opportunities to learn from one another. In a learning relationship that strives for mutuality and collegial patterns of working, addressing conflict deepens wisdom about self and others.

Many of our patterns of dealing with conflict have been learned in our families. One supervisee, Greta, insisted that her parents never argued. As an only child, she picked up an unspoken message that disagreement was not a good thing. In her teen years, she had a friend from a large family whose members argued and yelled at each other at top volume, or so it seemed to her. She liked the feeling of freedom in being able to express thoughts and feelings aloud, and she began to see that there were different ways to deal with conflict. Although she was not able to change the way her parents preferred to relate to each other or to her, she did learn to express herself more freely in friendships and more intimate relationships.

Becoming more aware of the patterns we learned while growing up helps us to become more aware of our own responses to conflict. This awareness may free us to look at other styles of conflict management. Although we may have one preferred way of dealing with conflict, I encourage those in leadership to develop a palette of styles, depending on the person and the situation. In general, I prefer to work cooperatively with others, yet at times I have needed to confront someone who was engaged in inappropriate behavior. I recall the tall, heavy-set young man in a youth group who thought it might be fun to bounce the bowling ball across the lanes. I told him to put down his ball, put on his coat, and go home. With surprise on his face that I would confront him about his behavior, he did just that. On another occasion, a chair of the board was angry and shouting at another board member. I quietly but firmly suggested that this approach was not appropriate, and that discussion about the issue might continue when tempers had cooled. Being confrontational is not easy for me, yet I have learned that some situations call for more assertiveness. Thus, I encourage supervisees to reflect on their preferred style of conflict management and to look at developing other styles.

Another layer of awareness about conflict that can be explored in supervision is identifying the nature of the conflict. Leas suggests that differences tend to focus on:

- facts
- methods

- goals
- values

Conflict can occur in a situation when understandings of the *facts* differ. Conversation to share information and verify facts can ease tension. When *method* is the point of conflict, procedures and strategies need to be spelled out. Sometimes when the *goal* is misunderstood, clarification of the objectives of a task is helpful. A higher level of misunderstanding occurs when conflicting *values* are at stake. Discussing what values we hold and why we hold them can move people toward resolution, yet such a process often requires much work and sensitive listening. Difficult as this discussion may be, taking time to thrash out the characteristics of the misunderstanding may prevent escalation to greater anxiety and a need for self-protection.

A further area of awareness in dealing with conflict is how it affects us personally. From a background as professor of congregational studies, James A. Sparks observes, "Criticism won't kill us but, as we all know from personal experience, it sure hurts."[6] Our most basic reaction to conflict is defensiveness, a feeling of vulnerability. In supervision, we are open to feedback and evaluation, comments that can range from affirmation for our brilliant work to suggestions for doing our work differently to outright criticism. Sparks offers a process to sort through the feelings stirred up by criticism when our defensive response is triggered, a process that may prove useful in a supervisory conversation.

Begin by choosing an occasion when you received criticism that triggered defensive feelings and that worried you afterward. You may select an incident from the past, allowing distance to offer some insights on how you react, or a more recent incident that provoked still-fresh feelings of defensiveness. Note on a piece of paper the following:

1. When the person spoke to you, how did you feel, how did you react physically, and what did you say?
2. Afterward, as you thought about the conversation, how did you feel, and how did you react physically?

3. Now, as you look back, how do you feel about what happened, and has there been closure to the incident?

Using this reflective process can be useful in sorting out our feelings, and in most situations, we may experience closure and perhaps be able to name valuable learning. However, some events generate deeper feelings that we are unable to let go of. Sparks outlines three dimensions to these feelings: trauma, brooding, and recovery.

Depending on the nature of the criticism and how it is delivered, we may experience a reaction that can only be described as *trauma*. Even if we have a relatively thick skin regarding criticism, we may be caught off guard if sensitive issues are triggered, or if we receive too many negative comments within a short space of time. When dealing with the trauma associated with criticism, Sparks suggests that rather than moving to defensiveness by justifying our actions or intentions, it is better simply to stay quiet and listen to what is being said. We need to attend to the comments as information rather than as complaint. This shift in perspective provides distance, so that we do not take the comments as a personal slight or outright attack. If the speaker is offering helpful feedback, then listening for information is important. If the speaker is working out his or her own anger and frustration, then we are listening for information about what is going on for this angry individual.

A second stage of defensiveness is *brooding*. In this phase we engage in self-blame, obsessing, and fantasizing. Self-blame takes the criticism and connects it to all our internal disapproving voices, sending us into a negative spiral. Whether the comments were minor or huge, we begin to blame ourselves for everything that has gone wrong and feel self-doubt that reduces our confidence. Obsessing deepens the self-blame, becoming a repetitive tape in our minds that will not go away, taking over all aspects of our lives. Part of this phase includes fantasizing about taking revenge, or quitting and finding another place to work, or in the case of what Sparks calls "people-intensive vocations," the fantasy of self-sacrifice. Leaders imagine that if they work harder and sacrifice more, people will like them better, and refrain from hurting them with criticism. The fantasy lies in the fact that we will never be able to work hard enough to please everyone.

This brooding phase has the potential to move us toward depression and an unhealthy perspective on life and work. To deal with this negative experience, we begin by acknowledging our feelings. If we made a mistake for which we are being criticized, then it is OK to feel upset, guilty, frustrated, or repentant. If the criticism is unjustified, feelings of anger and resentment are normal. We can express legitimate feelings directly to the person involved by returning to the conversation, if possible. We can find positive ways to affirm self-concepts and life such as physical activity, hobbies, lunch with friends, and meditation or prayer. Also, rather than brooding alone, stewing in our own juices, we can find a friend, supervisor, or professional to talk with and sort out what is going on in the situation both professionally and personally.

Recovery from this painful experience is evident when brooding recedes and when we are able to ask ourselves, "What have we learned from this incident?" If the criticism is justified, we may find information useful for our future ways of relating and working. Even if the criticism is unjustified, we can learn about the other person and his or her ways of being, about the way a faith community operates, and about our own emotional health and ways of dealing with critique. Through these experiences, we may deepen our self-knowledge and our wisdom about how to deal with future situations.

Communication and Conflict

In 1985 Edwin Friedman, rabbi and family therapist, popularized the term "triangulation" among church leaders. Used as part of the language of family systems theory, triangulation is an emotional triangle formed by any three people or issues. Friedman explains that "when any two parts of a system become uncomfortable with one another, they will 'triangle in' or focus upon a third person, or issue, as a way of stabilizing their own relationship with one another."[7]

Lots of relationships come in triangles that are not "triangulated." Triangle relationships are part of life, relationships such as mom, dad, and a child; or grandparents, parents, and grandchild; or one parent and two children. Triangle relationships are part of congregational life too, such as two paid staff and the chair of the board; or the incumbent clergy, the previous clergy, and the congregation; or two members of a committee and the chair. While triangles are formed within various relationships, *triangulation,* reminiscent of the rhyming word "strangulation," restricts the ability of a relationship to breathe and have life. A common example of triangulation in congregational life can be illustrated by a parishioner's comment to one clergy team member: "I really like Reverend Smith, but you are a much more dynamic preacher." The parishioner is trying to form an emotional bond with one of the pastors at the expense of the other. The parishioner needs to offer feedback or critique about Pastor Smith directly to her and not by taking sides with the other ministry staff. The same triangulation dynamics can occur among staff members. When faced with a teammate who somewhat blithely tried to triangulate many of my relationships in the congregation, I responded by moving out of the triangle. So, for example, when my associate said, "I think you have really upset the secretary with your innovative bulletin design," I responded by going directly to the secretary to discuss the bulletin with her. Often my teammate's critique was unfounded, and gradually he stopped trying to create such tension in the relationship.

Triangulated relationships are part of human connections, but they often diminish direct, honest communication. When conversation with others detracts from building positive relationships, triangulation is destructive. In an incident mentioned earlier, Deidre felt frustrated when Angus did not fulfill his responsibility to dispose of the flowers after worship. Deidre could have discussed her frustration about Angus with another person, thus triangulating the relationship, but she chose instead to address the issue directly with Angus, thus deepening understanding and mutual accord.

Triangulation is common in human interaction and becomes an issue for supervision, in which reflection on learning may include discussion of others and their behavior. Such discussion is useful if it leads to learning about self and others and offers insights into improved pastoral practice. A classic example in an internship: a congregation member approaches the student minister to talk about his or her issues with the pastor. Initially, the student minister may feel honored with such revealed confidences; however, such triangulation can erode the student-supervisor relationship. A suitable response is, "You need to speak to the senior minister directly rather than telling me." Triangulation is not limited to ministry staff; it can undermine all pastoral relationships. For instance, one worship committee member makes negative comments to another committee member about his dissatisfaction with the leadership of the worship chair. Continually talking *about* her to someone else rather than directly *with* her about the concerns undermines her leadership and disrupts honest communication. Talking with her directly about concerns offers an opportunity to work on issues and to find an amicable resolution.

To prevent triangulation, we need to be clear about what kinds of communication are acceptable and to encourage an environment in which people talk directly to one another. Leaders in a congregation can set the tone by communicating clearly themselves. When Homer, a newer member of the congregation, approached Deirdre in her role as worship chair because he was unhappy about the sermon on Sunday, she suggested that he speak directly to the minister, Bill. Homer did not know Bill very well and was nervous about talking with the minister. Homer thought Bill might get angry. Deirdre assured Homer that Bill was open to hearing responses to his sermons and offered to introduce him to Bill. Homer agreed, and what followed was an in-depth conversation between Homer and Bill. From that conversation, Homer felt confident in being able to offer future comments directly to Bill. They enjoyed getting to know each other, and each gained greater respect for the other's viewpoints.

To increase effective communication in a congregation, we need to establish norms for direct rather than indirect, or triangulated, conversation. We should not assume that people know how to avoid triangulating, so the board can discuss and establish norms for the pastoral team, the board, and all committees. These norms need to be posted clearly in a newsletter, displayed in the narthex or gathering place, and included in the annual report. Such norms become part of the framework for the supervisory relationship as supervisees are nurtured in their leadership roles. These norms are not simply positive ways of behaving with one another; they are part of living our faith through respectful and compassionate care of one another. Nonetheless, we should expect people to make mistakes as they learn different ways of communicating.

Friedman identifies other types of triangles, such as a "superpositive" triangle, in which the effusive praise of the new minister by a congregation member who is deeply disliked may be damming for the new clergy leader. Or there is the "vicarious" triangle. In this one, expectations for the minister are different from those for the rest of the congregation, as illustrated by such comments as, "Oh, we have an occasional drink ourselves, but we expect the minister to refrain from alcohol." Another type of triangulation with a much more undermining motivation is gossip, whether conveying truth or fiction. Talking about others is a human trait, and engaging in gossip can be enjoyable and often seems benign; however, gossip can at times betray boundaries. Phillip, a lay pastoral visitor, came to tell me that he had passed along information that he later realized was a betrayal of privacy. When visiting at the hospital, he recognized the name of a young woman on the visitors' list slated for day surgery. She was the daughter of the church secretary, Enid. Since Enid was his good friend, he called to let her know that he would be visiting her daughter. To his surprise, the secretary did not know her daughter was in the hospital, and further to his surprise, the daughter did not want anyone to know about the surgery. Even though confidentiality was a clear norm for all pastoral visitors, Phillip had not seen the need to maintain confidentiality, because he believed he was behaving compassionately in telling Enid he was visiting her daughter. Even though he was Enid's friend, he was obligated in his formal role as pastoral visitor to protect privacy; and he should have asked permission directly from Enid's daughter first.

Hearing the latest gossip can be seductive. If information is power, then learning about the latest scandal gives us a sense of power over others. Congregations can be hotbeds of hearsay, so learning positive ways to deal with this human tendency encourages more mature communication. Introducing the congregation's communication policy to new committee members, new board members, and new staff reinforces this preferred communication style with everyone. Supervisory conversations are occasions when issues of triangulation, confidentiality, and boundaries can be introduced, discussed, and explored using actual situations as case studies. Also, offering suggestions for effective communication increases people's resources. For instance, when a comment is made about another person, a response could be, "Perhaps you could speak directly to Pat. I know she will be interested in discussing this with you." Sometimes people are uncomfortable with direct conversation because of learned ways of relating. Perhaps a supportive supervisor might accompany an individual as he or she engages in this new relationship behavior. If the situation is fraught with strong feelings or the issues are complex, encourage the member to seek other ways of communicating, such as with the ministry and personnel committee, a group mandated to deal with delicate and conflict-laden issues in the congregation.

One further useful norm to establish is that no response will be given to anonymous letters. Hiding behind anonymity is spiteful and destructive, shutting down any possible communication, preventing resolution of conflict, and creating a sense of paranoia. Deirdre, as worship committee chair, often received spoken or written feedback about worship services. When she suddenly received a couple of malicious anonymous letters about one service that had dealt with a provocative issue, she was very upset. Deirdre took these letters to Bill, her supervisor, for advice on how to handle them. Bill suggested that the board develop a policy for dealing with such negative approaches to communication. The board's discussion resulted in Bill's announcement to the congregation during worship that anonymous communication would be ignored and not dealt with in any way. He went on to describe effective methods of communication available to congregation members who wished to express thoughts, feelings, and feedback.

Up to this point, we have been dealing with negative communication. However, positive or affirming comments are often not shared directly with others. In my family background, people did not tell each other that a task had been well done, for fear that the one complimented would get a "swelled head." In opposition to that family norm, I believe that offering affirmation develops self-confidence in an individual and creates a climate of encouragement in a faith community. Also, we may be more resilient in dealing with constructive criticism when we have a strong core of self-esteem. In addition, expressing appreciation for one another is part of offering positive feedback for a job well done, something all of us like to hear.

Narrative Mediation

An area of conflict resolution that is becoming popular in the legal system is mediation. Instead of paying huge sums of money for legal battles, the parties may bring in a mediator to help them find an amicable resolution. Mediation has a "problem-solving" approach[8] that is highly effective with conflict situations. Problem-solving, sometimes called "interest-based," approaches begin with the principle that people are motivated by their own self-interests. From this principle, the mediator encourages the conflicted parties to find common ground or shared interests not previously identified that both parties can agree upon. In this way, the parties can find a compromise solution without giving up anything.

Narrative mediation works from a different principle. Rather than assuming that people are working from self-interest, a narrative approach begins with the notion that people construe conflict from a narrative they create about the events. Mediation encourages the conflicted parties to change the way they see themselves within the conflict in order to entertain innovative possibilities for reconciliation. John Winslade and Gerald Monk are leading lights in this groundbreaking approach to conflict resolution. From their extensive mediation practice, they observe:

> The narrative approach is less grueling than problem-solving mediation, especially with long-standing conflicts. It concentrates on developing a relationship that is incompatible with conflict

and that is built on stories of understanding, respect, and collaboration. Parties are invited to reflect on the effects that these stories have had on them before they are asked to address the matters that cause separation. In this way, people move more quickly toward resolution.[9]

Narrative mediation may be of greater use in community settings such as congregations, where the narrative paradigm is part of the fabric of a faith community. We are "people of the story" as we connect our biblical story to our life stories in the ongoing chronicle of being in relationship with God. An initial premise in narrative mediation is not that we are problems that need to be solved but rather that we are people with a story to tell. Narrative mediation acknowledges "that people tend to organize their experiences in story form"[10] as they make meaning of their lives.

In narrative mediation, two people agree to work with a mediator, who may be a supervisor, to deal with the conflict in a respectful process of seeking a resolution helpful to both parties. In the process, both parties need to be agreeable to meeting and talking, and need to be committed to working toward a resolution. Narrative mediation will not be helpful with those who are not willing to talk with one another, or when one is afraid of the other. In an initial conversation, the mediator names norms for respectful conversation and ascertains the willingness of each party to talk and listen to one another. Listening to one another is not intended to elicit facts about the problem but to search for "how the story operates to create reality rather than on whether it reports accurately on that reality."[11] We know from experiences of listening to two friends who are in the midst of a disagreement that they will tell different stories about the discord, with varied perspectives on what took place. Spending time trying to find out the "truth" behind the stories will not be useful, as there is no ultimate truth to be found. Each person brings a particular version of what took place, viewing reality from his or her own perspective and worldview. We are listening for the impact of the situation on each person and what each desires as an outcome rather than trying to get to the bottom of what took place.

A narrative mediator encourages people involved in the conflict to tell the story of the conflict from their perspective in order to acknowledge how this story has given meaning and has affected their lives. For instance, as mentioned earlier, we can brood on issues arising from conflict, bringing self-blame, obsessing, and fantasizing—actions that have the potential to make us ill. From a narrative perspective, telling our stories enables us "to look for the narrow cultural and social prescriptions that constrain people's ability to view the options available to them."[12] We begin by listening to our own story, to be attentive to ways in which we construct meaning; and in reflecting on that story, we deconstruct the assumptions and values we brought to the story. From there we can imagine ourselves into new ways of being as we look at options that we previously could not contemplate because we were too fixed in our ways of thinking.

Narrative mediation invites us to listen to the story told by the other, as well as to our own story, not with the intent to set one person against another, or to determine who is telling the "truth," but to draw the parties closer to each other as they begin to appreciate the reality each one understands. Winslade and Monk observe:

> Ideally, narrative mediation is a cocreative practice in which the parties to the dispute are viewed as partners in the mediation. They are respected from the start because they possess local knowledge and expertise that can help bring about some form of resolution.[13]

Each person is an expert on his or her own life with a valid position in the relationship. From this positive relational approach, a spirit of understanding and compassion is created. Often, anxiety generated by conflict lessens as the parties have opportunities to tell their stories and to listen to one another in an attitude of respect, because they increase their sense of agency. Agency is the sense that we have control over our environment, the ability to be in charge of our lives. When conflict takes over our lives, we lose our sense of agency and believe that we cannot change what is happening. We feel powerless. As we listen to each other with respect, we can see the person as a complex individual rather than as a caricature created through the eyes of discord.

Conflict, as a natural part of all human relationships, is also a natural part of supervisory relationships. Rather than avoiding conflict, we can use opportunities to discuss our approach to conflict, to develop resources to deal with discord in supervision, and to strengthen our leadership skills.

FIVE

POWER AND SUPERVISION

Discussion of supervision cannot go far without an awareness of the place of power in the supervisory relationship, because power is invisible but present in all relationships. The topic of power is often avoided in relational conversations because of a common understanding that power is negative, abusive, hierarchical, and imposed. A quick glance at a thesaurus offers the following alternatives for the word power: authority, control, influence, supremacy, rule, command, clout, muscle, sway, dominance. These words indicate the typical images that come to mind when we hear the word power. However, power is neutral, neither negative nor positive. Power becomes good or bad in the way it is used, abused, received, and perceived.

In congregational life, many types of power are at work. We see the power of God's word, the power of the biblical story, and the power of religious symbol, for example. Relational power between the supervisor and supervisee begins with both personal and positional power. From her wisdom and experience as an adult educator, Patricia Cranton observes that personal power is based on "expertise, friendship and loyalty, and charisma. It is partly based on the personal characteristics of the individual and partly on the relationship the individual develops with others."[1] On the other hand, positional power is based on how people perceive a position of authority and on "formal authority, control over resources and rewards, control over punishment, control over information, and ecological or environmental control."[2] All relationships are a blend of personal and positional power.

In the early days of a pastoral relationship with a new minister, positional power takes the forefront because people don't know the minister's personality. But as time goes on and a relationship develops, personal power is more evident. When we listen to a sermon by a minister, we are listening with awareness of the speaker's positional power in her (or his) role as minister, as well as with awareness of her personal power, which depends on how well we know the pastor and what feelings we have toward her. At times, positional power and personal power can be in tension. I recall one instance when a congregation showed respect for the new minister because of the power of his position. As time went by and this minister alienated himself from the congregation with temper tantrums, backbiting, and lies, he eroded all personal power in the pastoral relationship. For a short time, people continued to show respect for his position, but as one person put it, "When I listen to him preach, the words are dry as dust and have no meaning for me." The positional power eroded to such a point that the board asked him to leave.

In a supervisory relationship, a supervisor has both positional and personal power—positional power through her role as supervisor and as a result of any other positions she may hold, whether as clergy, chair of the board, or chair of finance. A supervisor also has personal power based on individual qualities and the relationships she forms. On the other hand, the supervisee has power too. A supervisee definitely has personal power through the force of personal characteristics, the quality of gifts, and wisdom derived from life experience. And one has positional power through one's call to a designated office, whether as chair or member of a particular church committee. Often a supervisee relinquishes power because he perceives himself as having less expertise in his position as learner. However, the supervisor is a learner too. The principle that both supervisor and supervisee are learners is not just paying lip service to a desire for mutuality. Being co-learners is essential to fulfilling our ongoing call by God to share in Christ's ministry, to discern how to live that call continually, and to follow the leading of God's spirit. In a relationship between mutual learners, a quality of humility is created with shared respect and with openness to receiving gifts of insight and wisdom from each other. We can acknowledge what we know and the wisdom and expertise we hold at the same time that we have the humility to be open to new ideas and innovative directions, and are willing to have our assumptions challenged.

Power dynamics are part of any learning relationship because power is at the heart of a person's ability to learn. Learners need to feel within themselves the strength to approach the task of learning; they need to feel empowered from within to risk exploring, reflecting, growing, wrestling, discerning, and celebrating insights gained. Cranton declares that "an empowered learner is able to fully and freely participate in critical discourse and the resulting action; empowerment requires freedom and equality as well as the ability to assess evidence and to engage in critical reflection."[3] In my experience, those who do not claim that power within, that sense of empowerment, will feel too vulnerable to risk changing ideas, assumptions, previous ways of doing things, and belief systems. I have encountered many students who are so personally wounded that they fear having their beliefs and assumptions overturned by new ideas. They cling desperately to their worldview and resist what will feel like a paradigm shift. For these students to find the courage to learn, they will need to work with a counselor, therapist, or spiritual director to heal from within. Therapeutic work is a kind of learning, from an emotional and psychological perspective. When supervisory conversations veer into deep personal exploration, then the purpose of the conversation has shifted from learning to therapy, and the supervisee may benefit from a more explicit therapeutic relationship.

I have heard many leaders refer to their ministry as "empowering others." I can appreciate the desire to offer encouragement to others, but I am convinced that empowerment can come only from the inside out, from individuals claiming the power that is theirs. A leader or supervisor cannot empower another person. What a leader can do is to work to create an environment of mutuality and trust in which others can feel the courage to claim their power to learn and to minister in God's world. I had a conversation with a supervisee who was experiencing a great deal of conflict with a committee in the planning of an educational event. I asked her how she might describe her power as a leader in that setting. She quickly assured me that she did not have power. "I want to empower people, not have power myself," she declared. While I appreciated her desire not to exercise her leadership in an oppressive fashion, I believe that disavowing the power we have as leaders is debilitating personally and dangerous in our leadership. We all have power of one kind or another, and I find it preferable to name our understanding of power to be explicit about how we intend to use our power in relation to others.

Creating such an environment can be difficult, however, because we tend to treat power as a commodity: I have more power, but I will give some of that power to you. John Winslade and Gerald Monk have explored the concept of power in their work as conflict mediators. They propose:

> [P]ower does not so much adhere to structural positions in hierarchical arrangements as it operates in and through discourse. Discourses offer people positions of greater or lesser entitlement. Within particular discourses, some positions are rendered more legitimate or more visible and others are subjugated. Some voices get heard and others are silenced.[4]

Power operates in and through discourse, or the interaction and conversation that takes place in a relationship; thus power is relational, determined by the relationship dynamics. Power is not a fixed commodity but has fluidity dependent on the relationship. An executive with strong positional power as head of a company experienced very little power to influence his teenage daughter in their arguments at home. His power fluctuated, depending on the relationship involved. In another instance, a Native Canadian woman living on social assistance who often felt powerless in her social situation was invited to speak at a conference focused on issues in the native community. Suddenly, she found herself surrounded by people wanting to learn from her wisdom and experience. Unexpectedly, she had power to persuade and influence others in her shift from one social context to another.

As educators and supervisors, we hope to encourage the supervisee in learning. To create an encouraging environment, I find it useful to discuss the assumptions and expectations of the supervisory relationship. For instance, a supervisee may assume that a supervisor has more power because of greater knowledge and experience, and may expect words of wisdom and influence. For a supervisee, a supervisor's words will carry positional power, feel less-than-open to challenge, and be perceived more as instructions.[5] Supervisors need to be attentive to this dynamic in a learning relationship. However, trying to efface that power or using a commodity framework, imagining that power can be given away, will not be helpful. We need to view power as relational, as a force that will shift and change as the use of power is observed and discussed. As supervisors, we need to value the words of supervisees, their thoughts, feelings, and actions, to view them as people of agency, as able to effect change in their lives, as capable of claiming and accessing their personal and positional power.

The issue of expectations and assumptions of power in a supervisory relationship is not unidirectional. In a workshop I offered for supervisors, one highly respected minister with 35 years' experience in the pastorate spoke of how he felt intimidated by his supervisee. She was young, energetic, bright, working on a doctorate in theology, and full of innovative ideas for the congregation. I encouraged him to talk with the supervisee about his feelings, rather than distancing himself from her, as he had been doing. When he initiated that conversation, he discovered that the supervisee was totally surprised by his reaction to her. She had been feeling that she was in his shadow because of his long years of experience, his ease in presiding at worship and funeral services, the respect with which congregation members approached him, his pastoral wisdom, and his evident enthusiasm for congregational ministry even after 35 years. Laying out their assumptions about who had more positional and personal power allowed them both to share their gifts with one another and freed their relationship to grow in respect and trust.

Stages of Personal Power

As I observed earlier, I hope that a learning relationship will create
an environment in which learners feel a sense of agency and can
claim a sense of empowerment in their learning. One way to craft
that atmosphere is to be aware of where we are in our development
as people of agency. *Agency* is our sense of being able to act on our
own behalf, to speak up for ourselves, to claim our personal and
positional power. Agency is not an either/or commodity; it's a matter of degree. Janet O. Hagberg, in her extensive work as director
of the Silent Witness Initiative, has explored the concept of power
in her determination to eliminate domestic violence. Hagberg
suggests that six stages of power characterize individuals and organizations, moving from a feeling of powerlessness to a feeling of
empowerment. Stage 1 is a feeling of powerlessness:

> People feel trapped, angry, and unable to make things happen
> for themselves. They feel that things just keep piling up, and
> there is nothing they can do. They are, in a word, victims. They
> become dependent on others, and as a result they have low self-
> esteem. They are not actually trapped or helpless, but believing
> makes them so.[6]

In stage 2 people seek power by association, looking toward
others who seem to have more experience, agency, and ability to
cope. These people are seen as mentors, coaches, and teachers;
examples or models of ways to make more positive change. A
number of female theological students have found a greater sense
of agency in working with female supervisors, in seeing women in
ministry leadership.

People at stage 3 derive a sense of power through symbols and
achievement. A student minister, a young man with little sense of
power in his life, liked to wear a clerical shirt and collar because
it offered him a symbol of identity as minister that he did not feel
within himself. He worked hard at his studies, and upon graduation
and ordination he felt a greater sense of power from his achievement. Symbols and achievement offer people an external status that

they may not feel inwardly, from which they can "meet challenges, become assertive, and are willing to act. They strive for as much control as possible in life and in work."[7]

The movement from stage 3 to stage 4 is a movement from external to internal power. In this stage people are able to let go of a need to control, and personal ego is less at the forefront. Rather, people develop an ability to be present for and attentive to others' needs. Hagberg explains, "As they proceed through this stage, their sense of power emerges from the ability to touch others' lives by modeling integrity and sound judgment."[8]

As individuals moving toward stage 5, people demonstrate a further relinquishment of ego by embracing both strengths and vulnerabilities, so that a sense of purpose greater than themselves motivates their service to others.

In a final stage, 6, people access power through wisdom. This is the stage at which individuals operate from a more grounded place of wisdom. These people are simple yet complex, personally powerful yet apparently powerless. They fear nothing, and as a result they can act on principles that require deep courage. They are on the fringe and easily misunderstood, and yet they are highly respected by others. They are calm and peaceful inside, even when they are active or stressed.[9]

In this stage, people are able to rest comfortably in ambiguity or paradox when two seemingly contradictory ways of being are at work. Judson Edwards, noted Baptist minister and author, illustrates this ability well in his descriptions of leadership paradoxes. For instance, one leadership paradox is that the harder you try to control a group, the less control you will have. Edwards suggests that any attempt to be a strong and controlling leader "actually harms the conditions needed for strong leadership in a church—trust, respect, community, and laughter."[10] Instead, a person in stage 6 is able to offer leadership from a power based on an internal core that is strong and vulnerable at the same time, a leadership that is trusted.

For supervisors, our awareness of the stages of power will increase self-awareness of our own stage and how we use our power. In addition, that awareness will offer insights into the way supervisees are thinking and feeling about their own sense of power. In working with an accomplished youth-group leader, I found that he constantly deferred to me in every decision. I believed he was working from a stage 2 sense of power, looking to me as an authority. To continue working together, we needed to discuss the issue of power in our relationship. From that conversation, he began to claim his wisdom about youth-group leadership based on his experience and education in that area—wisdom I did not have. He began to grow in confidence and became more assertive in offering his ideas and challenging my assumptions about ministry with young people. Gradually we developed more mutuality in our supervisory relationship. We learned from each other and were enriched through shared wisdom.

Empowered for a Teaching Ministry

As congregational leaders, whether paid or unpaid, we need to ask: where do we get our power for leadership? We have personal power, and we are given power as leaders when we are authorized by God and the church. From a faith perspective, we find our power in and through God. God's grace poured forth freely and abundantly liberates us to share power with one another—not power over others in an oppressive fashion but a power that is respectful of self and others. In addition, there is an aspect of God's power demonstrated through vulnerability, even weakness. Philosopher and theologian Bernard Cooke has explored the dynamics of power in the working of God's Spirit. Theologies of the Christian Scriptures are quite clear: the God revealed in Jesus is not the support of those generally regarded as powerful, not the legitimation of patriarchal domination, but instead the God of the *anawim*, the poor and the powerless. It is not just that God protects and justifies the weak; in Jesus, God identifies with the "poor."[11]

As the embodiment of God's Spirit, Jesus demonstrates the power of powerlessness. Born in poverty, he had no official authority, no political or priestly office, or positional power. He had no wealth or economic power. Jesus demonstrated his power through the charisms of healing, teaching, and preaching. He was authorized to use this power by God's Spirit, and further authorized by the gathered community of disciples and faith-filled crowds. In the ultimate reversal of power, Jesus attains the highest status in our hearts, in our faith, and in our church through his absolute powerlessness in hanging on a cross. Cooke suggests that the greatest impact that Jesus has on our lives is in his confronting "the prospect of ultimate physical evil, death, and not allowing fear of that evil to deter him from total acceptance of his mission to overcome the more ultimate evil, sin."[12] Jesus shared with his disciples and shares with us the power to overcome fear through his trust in the power and love of God, his Abba.

In addition to being authorized to use our power through God's freely given grace, we also find positional power in being authorized by the church to heal, teach, and preach. One area important to supervision that is often overlooked in the church is God's call to a teaching ministry. Richard Osmer, the Thomas W. Synnot professor of Christian education at Princeton Theological Seminary, is passionate about the rediscovery and recovery of the teaching authority of the church.

> Rediscovery is the activity of discerning once again the meaning
> and power of a tradition that has been repressed and forgotten.
> Recovery goes further. It involves the positive evaluation and ap-
> propriation of that tradition, using what has been rediscovered
> to structure present patterns of thought and action.[13]

Recovery of the teaching office is not simply the construction of good Sunday school classes for children; it is the only hope for mainline churches. The teaching office is the essence and purpose of congregational life and focuses on three central tasks: (1) establishing the beliefs and practices of the church through denominational polity, mission statements, and congregational practices; (2) reinterpreting beliefs and practices in changing historical and cultural contexts; and (3) nurturing our sense of vocation as disciples of Christ so that each new generation can embody the gospel. This teaching authority is not a top-down, hierarchical approach, with the teacher holding the keys to knowledge judiciously imparted to a passive learner. The faith community as a whole is called, is authorized, to a teaching ministry in which all members are both teachers and learners; all members are invited by God to discover and recover the impact of God's love in their lives in a continual process of discernment. As Cooke advocates:

> Good teaching should be a joint effort at understanding by teachers and students. Knowledge of reality itself, not knowledge of the teacher's knowledge, should be the objective and norm of learning. The more basic power of education lies in the student's own thinking; the teacher acts as midwife.[14]

The image of teacher as midwife is a useful illustration of the supervisor's role as one who creates an environment where the birth of a deeper vocational clarity as disciples of Christ, whether for ordained or lay ministry, can take place. The teaching office of the church is not about handing down the tradition as a pure, unchanging package. Instead, teaching and learning in a faith community are about reclaiming the tradition anew as individual members interpret God's Spirit at work in their lives and community.   ·

Sources of Power

In a supervisory relationship, I ask supervisees to reflect on their understanding of power (see suggested framework below). What comes to mind when they hear the word *power*? Negative responses are typical, and people often name power as abusive, controlling, and oppressive. Initially most supervisees prefer to disavow any sense of power. When I was supervising Brad, a new chair of finance, we spent time discussing power as neutral and relational, and then reflecting together on our sense of personal and positional power. Brad began by naming his positional power in society that came from having a postsecondary degree, being a manager in a bank, having a relatively wealthy income, being male, and being heterosexual. He also had positional power in the congregation as a longtime member of the congregation and as the chair of finance. His personal power came from good mental and physical health, support of close family and friends, intelligence, physical size, and abundant life skills and coping strategies. Brad began to see that he carried a fair amount of power.

Questions for Reflection on Power

1. When you hear the word power, what thoughts, feelings, and memories are evoked?
2. Brainstorm sources of positional and personal power.
3. As you think back over your life, have you experienced any shifts in the sources of power or in the degree of power that comes from those sources?
4. In what ways do you acknowledge your power?
5. How does learning about power impact your understanding and expectation of supervision?
6. How might you deny or abuse your power in personal and professional relationships?
7. What is the impact of a conversation about power on the supervisory relationship?

To increase mutuality and trust in the supervisory relationship, a supervisor needs to engage in the same reflection. As supervisor I derive power in my position as minister and supervisor, from three postgraduate degrees, knowledge of the congregation, skills in ministry leadership, and theological education. My personal power comes from having confidence, experience, and good physical and mental health; being white; and possessing skills in teaching, writing, and praying. As we continue to talk about power in supervision, we need to acknowledge times when we might deny or abuse our power; doing so will allow us to increase our awareness of how we use our power in relationship with others. For instance, I cannot deny the positional power of being an ordained minister in a congregation. Rather, I can be aware that others might defer to my opinion, and be attentive to the thoughts and opinions of others, listening carefully and respectfully. More about abuse of power will follow in the next section.

The chart on sources of power and vulnerability may be helpful as you brainstorm about personal and positional power. In society, characteristics such as age and gender carry more or less power. From a postmodern perspective, power is not a commodity; rather, power is neutral and relational, personal and positional. However, in society, certain characteristics carry more power than others. A middle-aged adult has more agency than a child or an elderly person. Further, some social analysts would say that young adults carry more power in the consumer marketplace than older adults. Despite the progress of women's rights, males are still perceived to have a stronger position in society, although a black male carries less societal privilege than a white male. A person who is literate and has educational credentials has more power than those who do not. Many of these characteristics affect positional power in

Sources of Power and Vulnerability

Characteristic	Sources of Power	Sources of Vulnerability
Age	adulthood	youth, old age
Gender	male	female
Sexual orientation	heterosexual	gay, lesbian
Race	Caucasian	Asian, black, Native
Role	clergy	layperson
Physical stature	large size	small size
Economic status	stable & large income	poverty, lower income
Education	credentials	no formal schooling
Knowledge	information and knowledge	lack of information and knowledge
Psychological wellness	stability, support network	crisis, no coping skills, inexperience
Health	good mental and physical health	poor mental and physical health

society, yet they also affect a person's sense of self, his or her sense of personal power. For instance, a young man in the youth group from an upper-middle-class home with good physical and mental health, a strong network of family and friends, a deep sense of faith, and a quick intelligence had a learning disability that affected his ability to read. Illiteracy undermined his functioning at school and seriously compromised his self-esteem, his sense of personal agency. Once his learning challenge was identified and support was offered, he moved from a stage 1 sense of powerlessness to a stronger sense of agency, an ability to move forward with his education and life.

Abuse of Power

Discussion of power in the supervisory relationship has to include the abuse of power. In all areas of society, those with positional power have physically, sexually, psychologically, and emotionally abused those who are more vulnerable. When such abuse takes place within the church, a breach of trust occurs before God. In legal and theological terms, in a community of faith we enter a fiduciary relationship, a relationship of deep trust based on a compassionate and loving respect for one another framed by our understanding of God's gracious love and care for every human being in our churches, our communities, and our world. Breaching that trust is a travesty before God and obliterates the relationship between minister and congregation, and between congregation members. Although we hold the highest hope that our brothers and sisters in Christ will not breach that trust, we have to face the reality of our human frailty and the woundedness that causes us to sin. Consequently, a congregation must develop standards of behavior and practice that take into account both the temptation of sin and the vulnerability of those in our faith community.

Most denominations have created helpful resources to address abuse in congregational life, and every church board has a responsibility to make these resources available to all key lay leaders and members, as well as to set policies and procedures for standards of behavior for the faith community as a whole and as part of a supervisory relationship. Volunteer Canada is an organization that sets policies for volunteer groups—policies that have proved useful for all churches within Canada.[15] We have a "duty of care," a legal principle referring to the "moral, legal, ethical and spiritual obligation that one owes the other, especially the obligations to take reasonable measures to care for and protect the interest of the other. This obligation includes protection from harm such as sexual harassment, exploitation and assault."[16]

This duty of care requires that we set out clear expectations for people in all positions of responsibility in the church through screening individuals for those responsibilities to determine whether they have the necessary gifts, skills, experience, and desire for the position. Initial screening can include an application process, an interview, a reference check, and a police-records check. Ongoing screening may also include training, setting a probationary period, requiring supervision, doing random inspections, conducting regular evaluations, and offering clear policies about standards of behavior, as well as procedures that will be followed if those standards are not met. The level of screening is determined by the level of risk to those with whom the person will work. For instance, someone who will chair a breakfast club for men who gather once a month in the church presents a low level of risk for participants who are adult, able-bodied, and always in a group setting. Screening may involve an application or nomination process and an informal interview to determine willingness to serve and to discuss the responsibilities involved in the position. However, a church-school class for 3- to 5-year-olds that is legally classified as "vulnerable" presents a much higher risk; therefore, screening of prospective teachers may involve all of the above-mentioned elements.

Risk is assessed as low, medium, or high. Risk is low when a minister or lay leader has very little or no contact with children or vulnerable adults, and responsibilities are carried out in large groups. Medium risk involves work with vulnerable people when a pastor or care worker is never alone with anyone. Risk is high when a leader has opportunity to be alone with children and vulnerable adults and is able to exert influence over them. If the risk is high, supervisors need to make choices about how to reduce the risk. First, risk can be eliminated by canceling or rescheduling the activity. If only one youth group leader is available to take the group away for a weekend, then one option is to cancel or reschedule the activity for a time when more leaders are available. Second, if risk is high, a church may want to modify the activity. Rather than the choir director's giving private piano lessons at the church and spending time alone with children, the church may require a parent to be present during the lesson. Third, a congregation may lower risk by transferring liability. At Cross Street United Church, parents had been asked to drive teens to youth group events. Instead, a bus company was hired to transport the young people to some events, drawing on the training and insurance coverage of the company. Fourth, despite all risks assessed, a church may wish to assume risk fully because of the importance of the activity for the ministry and functioning of the faith community. A member of the congregation was a professional nurse who donated six hours per week to the church community for visits to the elderly or those in crisis. Working one-on-one with vulnerable people was classified as high-risk, yet the benefit to individuals seeking help was too important to lose, so the congregation included the nurse in its insurance coverage. Other ways to modify risk are to require that:

- All visits and counseling sessions be documented.
- A supervisor meet regularly with all leaders in high-risk positions.
- Meetings take place in the church in a designated office, preferably with another staff member present in the building.
- People do home visits as teams.
- Written parental consent be obtained for activities not in the church building.
- All leaders be active members of the congregation for one year before assuming responsibility in medium- and high-risk situations.
- All references be contacted.
- Further references be requested if needed.

- An experienced person work with a new person during an initial mentoring or probationary phase.
- Staff and volunteers undergo periodic training for responsibilities within their position.

Unfortunately, whatever precautions are established, risk cannot be eradicated. However, duty of care requires that faith communities assess risk in all leadership positions to make clear the standards for behavior with one another and to exercise legal, ethical, moral, and spiritual responsibility.

One element of screening that is used more frequently in the volunteer sector and that is beginning to be adopted in church circles is to request a police records check, a document supplied by the local police declaring whether an individual has a criminal record. Such checks have limitations, however. They are only as good as the day they are issued; they identify only those who have been caught committing a crime and do not name those who have been pardoned after a period of years; generally they do not require fingerprinting, which is a more reliable procedure for identification, and they produce a false sense of security. Also, depending on the jurisdiction, different levels of checks are available, and databases will vary. All that having been said, police records checks are an important element in the screening process in high-risk ministries, because such checks make clear to the faith community as a whole that the congregation takes the safety of its members seriously. Publicizing that checks are conducted may deter some people from taking on responsibilities for which they are unsuited.

In doing police records checks, be sure to have a clearly outlined policy for handling the paperwork. There may be state or provincial laws or denominational guidelines to assist in the development of such policies. In my denomination police record checks belong to the supervisee, so I simply acknowledge and record the date the document was issued and the date that I viewed it. This process avoids our having to come up with a confidential filing system for these sensitive documents. Some denominations require police records checks at regular intervals, such as every year, or every three

Sample Police Records Check Policy

Lay leaders of Cross Street United Church are in a position of trust; therefore, special care is taken to protect the vulnerable in our congregation through a process of screening. Initial screening includes an application process, an interview, reference checks, and a police records check. Ongoing screening includes successful completion of training, a probationary period, supervision, spot checks, regular evaluations, and clear policies about standards of behavior, as well as procedures that will be followed if those standards are not met. In positions of responsibility with high risk for those most vulnerable in our community, and in keeping with denominational policy, a police records check is required at the individual's expense and must be current within the last six months.

If a police record is found, there is no expectation that the individual will be stopped from holding a position of responsibility. What is expected is further conversation between the individual and a person designated by the ministry and personnel committee on behalf of the board to discuss the impact of the criminal record in light of a risk assessment of the position. All risk assessments for all congregational positions are available for review in the congregational handbook.

In the interests of confidentiality, the police records check will be the property of the individual and will not be in possession of any member of the congregation or paid staff. Such a check will be viewed by members of the ministry and personnel committee, with the date of the check noted in the personnel records. In addition, this police records check will be treated with utmost confidentiality, and information gleaned from viewing its contents will not be shared either in conversation or in writing beyond the ministry and personnel committee.

years. Also, a congregation needs to be clear, before it begins conducting checks, about what to do when a conviction is revealed in
the police records check. Rather than refusing a potential candidate
for a position, church officials need to discuss with the supervisee
the implications of having a criminal record for the position he or
she has applied for. Sex-related crimes may be grounds for barring
an applicant from consideration for a position of responsibility,
whereas a minor drug-related offense from 20 years ago with no
other convictions may not preclude a candidate from being part
of a teaching team for a church-school class. This conversation can
take place between the supervisor and supervisee, or with one or
more members of the ministry and personnel committee.

Regardless of the specifics of the learning covenant and the
learning goals of a supervisee, supervision is another important
element of ongoing screening. Training for responsibilities, establishing transparent standards of practice, and providing feedback
and performance evaluation all contribute to a congregation's duty
of care, both to those most vulnerable and to the person taking on
a leadership responsibility.

Spiritual Abuse of Power

Although churches are becoming more aware of abuse of power
through physical, emotional, psychological, and sexual harm,
most congregations have, oddly enough, given little consideration
to spiritual abuse. David Johnson and Jeff VanVonderen, in their
work respectively as minister and therapist, have explored spiritual
abuse as another element in our duty of care. They define spiritual
abuse as treatment of an individual that wounds or scars his or her
capacity to be in relationship with God.[17] When people are vulnerable, needing support or spiritual nurture, and a leader weakens,
undermines, or decreases an individual's spiritual agency, then
abuse has occurred.

In defining spiritual abuse, Johnson and VanVonderen offer
some distinctions. A spiritual leader is not abusive when making
responsible leadership decisions using his or her best judgment
and abiding by the polity of the denomination and the transparent policies of the congregation. Sometimes those decisions may

be contrary to individual members' opinions. However, using a difference of opinion to devalue a person's spirituality is abusive. Also, correcting a person's behavior is not abusive if framed within the transparent polity of the denomination in a desire to heal and reconcile, as opposed to shame or discredit. Asking a person to step down from responsibilities because of his or her emotional, physical, mental, or spiritual health is not abusive if the request follows congregational policies of duty of care for the congregation and the individual. Disagreeing with someone about theological beliefs or doctrines is not spiritual abuse so long as the discussion is respectful and not belittling. Setting standards for behavior is not abusive so long as no one is spiritually degraded or shamed because she or he does not adhere to that standard. Congregations aren't perfect, and feelings get hurt. In a spiritually healthy environment, however, talking about problems, hurt feelings, and systemic abuses is permissible. Spiritual abuse occurs when individuals are made to feel spiritually lacking or outside God's love and care because they question policies or point out problems. Johnson and VanVonderen point out elements of an abusive system:

1. **Power posturing.** A leader spends a great deal of time and energy focused on developing and maintaining his or her own power and authority.

2. **Performance Preoccupation.** Along with power posturing among leaders, a congregation is consumed by the performance of its members. Obedience to a legislated authority and submission to leadership decisions is expected.

3. **Unspoken rules.** Rather than setting transparent policies and making them available for all members to read and understand, spiritually abusive systems control people's lives through unspoken rules. Members do not know the rules until they break them; and having broken a rule, an individual, rather than any shortcoming in the regulation, is identified as the problem. In some churches, individuals are silenced or eliminated as punishment for breaking a tenet.

4. **Lack of balance.** An unbalanced approach to living our faith is shown in two extremes: extreme objectivism and extreme subjectivism. An extremely objective approach "elevates objective truth

to the exclusion of valid subjective experience,"[18] creating a system dependent on a level of education and intellectual capacity alone. On the other end of the spectrum, extreme subjectivism gives huge emphasis to feelings and experiences of God's revelation, usually received by the leader and imparted to the followers.

5. Paranoia. A paranoid system is a closed society in which a few enlightened leaders hold the secrets to the faith. Others outside the enclave will not understand, because they are not enlightened. Paranoia is demonstrated when the closed system maintains strong boundaries against others to protect itself, in a belief that others will respond negatively to the system.

6. Misplaced loyalty. In a spiritually abusive system, disagreement with the leaders is seen not only as disloyalty but also as disobedience to God. Loyalty is bolstered by the assumption that the leaders alone are right. Members must stay in the system if they are to be spiritually safe. Leaving the congregation puts their salvation at risk. Scare tactics may be used, such as threatening or actually humiliating a person by public shaming, or threatening removal from the group.

7. Secretiveness. Keeping confidence within clearly outlined guidelines and policies for the good of the community and vulnerable individuals is not the same as secret-keeping in which power is cloaked in secrecy and vulnerable individuals are put at risk when information concerning the health and welfare of a vulnerable individual is kept secret. Secrecy is vital in a rigid system that needs to control others.

When the elements cited above are present in a faith community, the congregation is likely suffering spiritual disease typified by what Johnson and VanVonderen describe as:

> a closed system, with rigid boundaries that prevent people from leaving. There will be the perception of a lot of evil on the outside, to keep people in, and there will be a lot of power postured on the inside to compel you to perform. There will also be tired, wounded people who feel that they are either unspiritual or

crazy. And they will have major problems relating to God from the heart.[19]

Power in a healthy congregational system needs to be discussed openly to develop trust in supervisory relationships. Johnson and VanVonderen observe:

> Trust is not something that can be demanded or legislated. It is gained or lost on the basis of integrity and honesty. People who say what they mean and live consistently with their ideals are people you can trust, and more consistency is required of spiritual leaders as a demonstration of spiritual authenticity.[20]

Integration of what people say and how they behave creates trust. No one is perfect. And no one can be expected to live a perfect life. Yet even open discussion of imperfection demonstrates and increases spiritual authenticity, important for all partners in a supervisory relationship. Power is invisible, but its impact is felt in all relationships. Raising awareness of our personal and positional power is an important aspect of our supervisory relationships as we learn to share power and be attentive to situations in which we may abuse the power God has given to us.

SIX

ENCOURAGING THE LEARNING COMMUNITY

I believe that whether clergy or lay, paid or unpaid, everyone in a key leadership position needs to be a lifelong learner, both as part of one's own personal development and as part of an ongoing nurture of Christian faith. Leaders who are energized by their faith and their commitment to service in the church will be inspiring to the whole church community. Developing an encouraging learning environment for members and in particular for paid staff and key lay leaders is part of a congregation's call to ministry leadership.

Learning Covenant

In introducing the concept of a learning covenant, a minister can begin with the key lay leaders, those who are chairs of committees. Assuming that the congregation's board is composed of its committee chairs, discussion of learning covenants and exploration of learning goals can be part of a church board meeting. Committee chairs or paid staff could then introduce learning covenants to committee members.

Because supervision is about learning, the learning covenant is at the heart of the supervisory relationship. Supervision is a relationship in which both supervisor and supervisee are focused on nurturing their leadership gifts within congregational ministry—formation for ministry leadership. A learning covenant is an agreement about what people want to learn and any other pertinent information such as length of relationship, position description, conflict-management procedure, sexual abuse and harassment policy, and so on.

In adult education the term "learning contract" has been used to describe a formal learning agreement between two parties. However, the term "covenant" has been used in theological education and in church life when talking about a learning contract because we associate "covenant" with God. The word covenant conjures up biblical images of God forming relationships with the people of Israel, from God's hearing their cries to be released from slavery in Egypt to God's offering the commandments that shaped their life as a faith community on Mount Sinai and beyond. As Christians, we have a sense of covenant with God embodied in the life, ministry, death, and resurrection of Jesus, God's gracious spirit made flesh. While covenant has a contractual element, in faith communities covenant is used to mean that we are bound together as people of God. Within a covenant we are accountable to one another and to God.

R. E. Y. Wickett is a professor in the department of educational foundations, University of Saskatchewan, with an interest in learning covenants. He names principles essential to developing a learning covenant with adult learners, principles that are usefully adapted in a supervisory relationship.[1] Both supervisor and supervisee are self-directed learners able to:

- name their own areas of learning
- plan and implement the learning process
- evaluate their learning
- bring closure to the learning relationship

While a supervisee may have less experience than the supervisor, the supervisee brings life experience and interest in a learning area to the relationship. Interest and motivation in adult learners are higher when they are able to identify their own learning aspirations rather than having a goal imposed upon them. As adult learners, supervisees are invited to name what they would like to learn and, in conversation with the supervisor, develop a plan. A supervisor can also offer tools for developing learning goals and reflecting upon and evaluating the learning. Finally, a timeline for the learning goal is useful. If the leadership term or appointment is for an extended period—for instance, two years—the learning covenant can be renegotiated each year, with the possibility of deepening the learning from the previous year, or developing a new area of interest.

A supervisor is a learner alongside the supervisee, also naming learning goals for herself, goals that might include development of supervisory gifts such as active listening and theological reflection, or development of leadership abilities in areas that need further refinement. In addition to being a mutual learner, a supervisor brings gifts of facilitating the learning of the supervisee by offering a framework for developing the learning covenant along the lines of Wickett's principles, which include:

- a structure for developing learning goals
- resources to implement goals
- tools for reflection
- an evaluation process

Within a congregational setting, a learning covenant can be viewed as an opportunity for growth in personal Christian faith, in leadership gifts, and in leadership formation, as well as in other arenas. For learning to be successful, a supervisee needs to feel that he has learned something significant and found satisfaction in the learning process, so care needs to be taken in creating learning goals and devising a strategy to implement those goals. Paying lip service to identifying a learning focus at the beginning of the church year and then never meeting with a supervisee or holding the supervisee accountable for the learning will result in dissatisfaction. Also, resources or access to resources needs to be provided. Resources can include books, articles, films, Web sites, workshops, spiritual direction, prayer, group discussion, interviews, journal-keeping, and ministry-site visits. Learning is further enriched if time is taken for reflection on learning, using both conversation and written expression. A supervisor can introduce these tools early in the supervisory relationship. And finally, evaluation needs to be an ongoing part of learning. Learning can be conceived as a spiral that begins with naming an area of interest, deciding how to explore that interest, doing the exploration, reflecting on what happened, and identifying insights and learning. A basic evaluative question is, "What have you learned?" From those insights, further learning goals may be established. Learning is not stationary. Rather, learning evolves from action through reflection to new action, further reflection, and so on. More will be said about evaluation in chapter 7.

Learning Goals

A learning covenant can include individual or group goals. For instance, a Christian education committee was interested in moving away from the traditional model of Sunday school toward a learning-center model for the children's Sunday gathering, so the group created a goal to research and develop a learning-centered teaching environment. Within that large group goal, individual members agreed to research aspects of the goal that caught their interest. Time was allotted in each Christian education committee meeting to reflect on the learning as it progressed throughout the year.

On the other hand, the worship committee was more interested in exploring individual goals. Deirdre, as chair, wanted to learn more about conflict management, feeling sure that this skill would enhance her leadership gifts. She had already explored some resources: a book she wanted to read and a course being offered by the denomination. A committee member, Jack, a longtime member of Cross Street, wanted to learn more about prayer, both the distinct types of prayer used in worship services and elements of his own personal prayer life. Sally, a mother of three young children and new to church life, wanted to understand the traditions behind the liturgy. As a leader in the youth group as well as a worship committee member, Claire wanted to focus on how she could involve youth in more worship services, perhaps through reading Scripture, dramatizing biblical stories, and leading more contemporary hymn singing. With her own love of worship, she wanted to draw more young people to church on Sunday morning through their direct participation in the service.

Sample Learning Covenant

As part of my service to Cross Street United Church, I agree to develop my leadership gifts and to nurture my vocation as one called by God to serve the church locally and globally.

Name: _____

Position: _____

You may wish to include contact information such as phone number, e-mail address, and mailing address.

Timeline: *(start date)* until *(conclusion date)*

General Agreements

Supervisor and supervisee agree to meet _____ *(weekly, bi-monthly, monthly)* to reflect on current ministry experiences arising from the learning goals.

- Supervisees will evaluate their learning at regular intervals *(agree on specific dates, perhaps midway and toward the end of the learning period).*

- If supervisees encounter conflict within their leadership responsibilities, the supervisor must be notified to initiate congregation's conflict procedure as appended.

Congregational and denominational policies on conflict, sexual abuse and harassment, and respectful communication apply to all individuals in leadership positions. I have read and understand the policies.

Supervisee: _____

Supervisor: _____

Date: _____

The learning goals are attached to this covenant.

Interns are expected to select a number of learning goals that may include goals suggested by their theological college, their judicatory, and their supervisor, as well as goals they have identified for themselves. Goals usually span a number of areas to address leadership formation—such as identity as a minister, ability to relate to people of varying ages, theological reflection, spirituality, and such ministry skills as preaching, visiting, administration, and teaching. In a full-time congregational internship, an intern has opportunities to explore a number of goals addressing personal, spiritual, and vocational development.

Over the years as a supervisor, I have engaged in many conversations about developing the perfect learning goal. Some supervisors spend a great deal of time crafting a goal with a supervisee; meanwhile, useful learning time is slipping past. My preference is quickly to identify an area of learning, with the understanding that learning will deepen with experience, feedback, theological reflection, and evaluation. Beginning with the seemingly simple task of learning how to pray may engage the learner in deeper reflection on the efficacy of prayer, the theological assumptions behind prayer, and the intuitive prompting of God's Spirit during prayer. Beginning with what seems an abstract question about the efficacy of prayer might lead a learner to pray. At whatever point a learner chooses to engage, whether with a task, a skill, or a meaning question, learning is explored and deepened in the supervisory conversation.

In my experience, people enjoy learning about topics that interest them. However, with the best of intentions, they often find that they don't follow through on that learning. Setting a learning goal assists that follow-through by creating a plan for learning and accountability for that learning with others and with God. The following model offers a structure for creating a plan and for building in accountability. This model does not need to be followed slavishly; nonetheless, it does offer a series of questions to stimulate thinking about a goal. Some goals are broad and benefit from sequenced steps that break the goal into separate objectives and tasks. Other goals are already precise and task-oriented, so that learners may not need to follow all the outlined steps.

Developing a Learning Goal

Identify a Learning Goal

Ask yourself: what would I like to learn?

Example 1: From a member of the worship committee: "I want to learn more about worship."

Example 2: From a member of the youth and young adult committee: "I want to learn how to involve more youth in worship."

Develop Objectives

Ask yourself: what are some *specific* ways to work on the learning focus?

Example 1: "I will reflect on what happens during our own Sunday service. I will ask the worship committee to discuss the parts of the service and their meaning. I will identify resources to learn about worship in my denomination. I will look at resources from other denominations."

Example 2: "I will attend youth group meetings to discuss worship participation. I will find a list of youth who are part of the church but do not attend youth group meetings for a wider discussion."

Plan Your Actions

Ask yourself: what actions do I need to initiate to make this happen?

Example 1: "I will look for resources on worship. I will find copies of previous Sunday bulletins to identify the structure of worship. I will ask the worship committee for time at one of their meetings."

Example 2: "Find out youth group meeting schedule and ask for time during a meeting for conversation about worship participation. Consider questions to ask youth to determine their interest in worship participation and what kind of participation. Send questions to youth who do not regularly attend youth group meetings. Ask for time at a worship committee meeting to discuss the possibilities for youth participation."

Choose Resources

Ask yourself: what resources will I need?

Example 1: "Ask secretary for bulletins from other Sundays. Check out resources in the church library. Look on the Web for denominational resources on worship. Explore worship resources from other denominations. Enjoy discussion with the worship committee."

Example 2: "I will need to develop questions for my meeting with the youth group, in consultation with one or two other youth. I will need to deliver or mail questions to those youth who do not attend youth group. I need a list of youth in the church from the church secretary. I need to contact the chair of worship to book time at a worship committee meeting."

Reflect on Your Learning

Ask yourself: how will I reflect on what I have learned?

Example 1: "I will share my research with the worship committee. I will reflect with my supervisor, the chair of worship."

Example 2: "I will debrief insights from my visits to the youth group, my attendance at a worship committee meeting, and my responses from other youth with my supervisor, the youth group director."

Acknowledging My Learning

Ask yourself: how will I know that I have learned?

Example 1: "I will feel greater confidence in my work on the worship committee."

Example 2: "I will have a clearer sense of how to include youth in worship. I hope that some young people will have a greater interest in attending worship."

A learning goal can be task-oriented, focused on a particular project, such as Claire's desire to incorporate youth participation in worship services, or it can be more abstract—for example, "I want to deepen my faith in God." People may have all kinds of interests they wish to pursue, but for the purpose of a learning covenant, the learning goal should be related to the work and life of the congregation and, if applicable, the particular committee. Each congregation will need to decide the level of accountability for the learning that takes place. Paid staff may be required to set learning goals for each year, whereas key lay leaders may be invited, but not required, to set goals. For instance, a ministry and personnel committee that oversees the work of all paid staff may require annual learning goals as part of a yearly review. The ministry and personnel committee may fulfill the role of supervisor, or may assign a member of the committee or another designated person to supervise. Janice, a member of the ministry and personnel committee, works from home and is willing to meet with the church secretary once a month to review the secretary's work and learning goals. Janice reports back to the committee at their regular meetings on how the secretary is doing in her work, particularly areas of satisfaction and areas of frustration. On the other hand, Deirdre, in her role as worship chair, serves as liaison between the ministry and personnel committee and Yun Sung, the church organist. Deirdre offers brief but regular reports to the ministry and personnel committee on her meetings with Yun Sung.

The board may expect all committee chairs to develop learning goals as part of their formation for this leadership position. Supervision, as opportunities to reflect on learning goals, can be offered by a minister or other staff person who can check in with committee chairs on a rotating basis once a month. In turn, committee chairs can create an environment for committee members to develop and explore a learning focus. Reflection on learning can take place during committee meetings, or that aspect of supervision may be offered by other lay leaders, clergy, or staff, depending on the learning goal. For instance, Claire, a young person and member of the youth and young adult committee, is being supervised by the youth group director because of her interest in including young people in the worship service.

Position Description

Another aspect of leadership formation is clarity of role and responsibility for all staff, committee chairs, and committee positions. Anyone beginning a new position benefits from having expectations laid out clearly. Typically, congregations are not attentive to creating position descriptions for paid staff, let alone for those who volunteer their time.

Many denominations offer a process for developing position descriptions for paid staff. Within my own denomination, a brief document offers a process for creating a position description in preparation for hiring or calling a new staff person.[2] Consider the following areas in developing the position description:

- Clearly outlined responsibilities, including frequency of performance and time to be spent.
- Duration of commitment.
- Skills required.
- Training provided.
- Identification of areas of sole responsibility and areas that require teamwork and consultation.
- Inclusion of policies that will affect work, such as congregational policies on weddings and baptisms, conflict resolution, and sexual abuse and harassment procedures.
- Date of position description and date for review.

As part of clarifying the position description, human resources consultant Erwin Berry recommends a procedure for welcoming all paid staff to a congregation that includes greeting, dealing with employment forms, touring the work areas, and reviewing all employment regulations including evaluations and merit increases, work safety, continuing education, and regular performance feedback.[3] Having an orientation procedure for

Sample Position Description for Paid Staff

Title: Ordained Minister of Worship and Pastoral Care
Role: to work in a team with the minister of outreach and Christian nurture and the congregation.
Responsibility: The minister will lead planning, preparation, and implementation of worship within the mission of Cross Street United Church and the denominational polity, and will offer pastoral care and spiritual nurture to all members.
Accountability: The minister is directly accountable to the board of Cross Street United Church through the ministry and personnel committee.
Ministry Gifts: A person in this position will be a member of the denomination in good standing, able to articulate his or her faith, and will adhere to the polity of this denomination and of Cross Street United Church. In addition, such a person will bring strengths in interpersonal communication, conflict management, preaching, organization, and compassionate listening; will exercise clear boundaries; and will demonstrate a desire to express the love of God in this faith community.

Expectations

Principal Duties:
1. The minister will work with the worship committee, other staff, congregation members, and the choir in offering relevant, inclusive worship each Sunday. This responsibility will include preaching; presiding at worship, communion and other sacraments; performing baptisms upon request and within the policies of Cross Street United Church; attending worship committee meetings, and other meetings as required for preparation of worship, such as meeting with families of children who are to be baptized.
2. The minister will work in a team with the lay pastoral visitation committee, other staff, and congregation members in offering ongoing and crisis pastoral care and spiritual nurture. This responsibility will include doing hospital visitation, visiting shut-ins, and responding to pastoral concerns of congregation members, as well as conducting funerals and seeing to their preparation. In addition, this responsibility includes attendance at lay pastoral visitation committee meetings to offer ongoing support and education for the pastoral care ministry.
3. The minister has sole responsibility for congregational administration, including consultation with the chair of the board to develop a yearly mission focus at Cross Street United Church. Administration also includes responsibility for the weekly staff meetings, and supervision of learning goals of all board committee chairs.

Additional duties include:
1. Attendance at all monthly board meetings.
2. Facilitation of weekly staff meetings.
3. Attendance at ministry and personnel committee meetings upon request.
4. Preparation and presiding at weddings of church members only.
5. Attendance at presbytery, conference, and wider church meetings, in consultation with the ministry and personnel committee.

Time Required

The following is a guide for carrying out the duties cited above, not as a document to be followed slavishly but as a description of the weight given to responsibilities assigned.
- Worship preparation: 13 hours per week.
- Pastoral Care: 8 hours per week.
- Prayer, study, and reflection: 4 hours per week.
- Commitments to the wider church: 4 hours per week.
- Board meetings: 3 hours per month.
- Supervision of all board committee chairs: 3 hours per month.
- Staff meetings: 2 hours per week.
- Reflection with assigned supervisor: 2 hours per month.

Vocational Formation
Time and financial support are offered each year for ongoing leadership formation through continuing education. Formation will be enhanced through development of a learning covenant, reflection on the covenant, and year-end evaluation with a supervisor who is a member of or liaison to the ministry and personnel committee.

Resources for Learning
A budget of *(amount)* and three weeks' continuing education per year is available. A library of worship resources is available, as well as a budget of *(amount)* for purchase of personal books and resource materials. Additional financial support for leadership-development courses specific to the nurture of leadership gifts at Cross Street United Church is available upon request to the ministry and personnel committee.

Screening Procedure
Given the high-risk assessment of this position, a police records check will be required every three years.

Review of Position Description
This position description will be reviewed annually in conversation with the ministry and personnel committee, with changes to be recommended to the board.

the first day of a new position reduces employee anxiety and demonstrates care for the staff and ultimately the congregation. To assist a congregation in establishing helpful employment policies, Berry offers samples that cover procedures such as fair treatment of employees, discipline, leave of absence, salary and performance evaluation, performance goals, working conditions, and exit interviews.[4] Berry also suggests that congregations create an employee handbook that includes a welcome, brief history of the congregation, mission statement, personnel philosophy, employment information, work schedule, payment schedule, performance evaluations, leaves of absence, benefits plan, sexual harassment and substance abuse policies, termination policy, and work safety. And just to make sure that no one can say he or she did not see the handbook, a further sample "Employee Handbook Acknowledgement" asks a new employee to sign a statement saying, "I have received, read, and understand the contents of the Employee Handbook."[5] While these policies may seem to be a huge shift in some congregations' present ways of working, Berry suggests that creating such policies is part of maintaining good order in the congregation:

> A quick look at a biblical concordance will not find the phrase "personnel policies and procedures" in any of the 27 New Testament books. What any study of the New Testament will find, however, are a plethora of references to structuring the body of Christ so that the Good News of Jesus Christ can be communicated most effectively. In the modern world of the church, this undoubtedly means efficient, effective, and fair staff relations. Paul's admonition to the Corinthian church that "all things be done decently and in order" (1 Corinthians 14:40)—although speaking of a particular issue related to that community's worship—is also a mandate to those who are in positions of responsibility within a congregation to establish a clearly defined and understood set of staff policies.[6]

Just and fair treatment of employees that includes clearly defined expectations is not just good organizational policy; it is a way to embody the gospel. The hope is that contented staff members will offer stellar work.

A similar process is useful when lay leaders take on unpaid, volunteer positions of responsibility. Even though there are no employment procedures, taking time for orientation to new duties expresses care for the lay leader, ensures appropriate continuation of previous efforts, encourages a standard for performance of duties, and establishes accountability. A ministry and personnel committee or a nominations committee might outline the position description for committee chairs for approval by a congregation's board. Within each committee, position descriptions can be developed for particular roles. For instance, the financial stewardship committee has position descriptions for the chair, treasurer, stewardship campaign chair, and offering captain. The following is an example of what might be developed for a chair of a worship committee.

At Cross Street United, support staff do the work outlined in their position descriptions. Communication between the ministry and personnel committee and staff is enhanced by having a lay leader supervise the work of a staff person. In his role as chair of the property committee, Stanley checks on the day-to-day work of the custodian, Everett, for support and accountability. Everett likes to have his work clearly spelled out down to the last detail, so that he knows exactly what he needs to do each day. Stanley often meets with the custodian to discuss how to do repairs and maintenance of the church building. Everett has been custodian for 14 years and although not a fastidious cleaner, he never misses a day of work, is punctual, and is friendly with everyone coming in and out of this busy church building. While Stanley gives Everett clear instruction about tasks that need attention, Stanley also offers support to Everett by recommending to the board a yearly thorough cleaning of the whole building by a commercial cleaning company. Stanley reports to the ministry and personnel committee about ongoing progress as well as any concerns raised by the staff.

Relationships between lay leaders and committee members are of a voluntary nature rather than paid, but nonetheless, clear expectations are just as important. An active member of the church

Sample Position Description

Role: Chair of worship committee

Responsibility: A chair of the worship committee will facilitate monthly meetings of the worship committee with the purpose of developing worship services in coordination with ministry staff in light of the mission of Cross Street United Church and the denomination.

Accountability: The chair of the worship committee is directly accountable to and a member of the board of Cross Street United Church.

Ministry Gifts: A person in this position will be a full member of the congregation with a demonstrated faith and love of worship. Gifts of communication, organization, and desire to include the whole family of God in worship will be an asset.

Expectations: The worship committee chair will facilitate the monthly worship committee meetings, attend monthly board meetings, attend worship regularly, and be available for consultation with ministry staff. In addition, the chair will prepare quarterly "Worship Corner" reports for the church newsletter, and an annual congregational report. The chair will also supervise the organist in developing goals for his or her learning, ensure that time and money are set aside for continuing education, encourage the musician to take advantage of learning opportunities, and be a liaison to the ministry and personnel committee upon invitation.

Time Required
- Worship committee meeting preparation and facilitation: 3-4 hours per month.
- Board meeting preparation and facilitation: 3 hours per month.
- Attendance at worship: 2 hours per week.
- Consultation with ministry staff: 1 hour per week.
- Supervision of organist: 1 hour per month.
- Reflection with assigned supervisor: 1 hour per month.

Position Period: This is a two year position, renewable for an additional year.

Vocational Formation: Leadership formation will be enhanced through development of a learning covenant that consists of developing a learning goal for the year, engaging in reflection on the learning goal, and completing an end-of-year evaluation with a supervisor.

Resources for Learning Goals: A budget of *(amount)* is available for the work of the worship committee, including purchase of resources for leadership formation of the chair and all members. A library of worship resources is available to ministry staff and the worship committee. Financial support for leadership-development courses specific to the work of the worship chair may be requested from the ministry and personnel committee.

for 50 years and a management consultant in his work life, Rick Curry brings a wealth of experience to his observation that "the health of a thriving church community depends not only on the many ministries performed, but also on the administration that underpins them."[7] Curry offers guidelines for structuring church committees, along with expectations for individual committee members. Committee members are accountable to the congregation as a whole through the church council or board. Formal relationships with responsibilities and accountability need clear expectations and support. Often committee chairs and members are unclear about what is expected in these positions, and expectations are left up to an individual chair's gifts, time, and energy. Rather than simply leaving the establishment of clear expectations to the goodwill of a committee chair, a church board needs to take responsibility through the ministry and personnel committee for clarifying all roles and responsibilities in voluntary positions.

Betty agrees that developing clarity is important. As newly elected chair of finance, she has oversight of committee members who have clearly outlined duties such as managing church accounts and overseeing the stewardship campaign. Betty was troubled when she discovered that counting the collection on Sunday morning was poorly organized. Counting teams were not arranged with enough notice; often one person was left to count alone, creating a long and cumbersome task. Aside from an issue of good stewardship of time, Betty was concerned about protecting church money and an individual counter's reputation. Responsibility for this faith community's offering to God is a sacred trust. The board is accountable to the congregation for the process of collecting money given for the work of the church and community during worship, and for providing a trustworthy counting and banking system. To formalize the position of counter and to offer clear expectations, Betty created an "offering captain" position with a clear description. She developed a yearlong roster of counting teams, as well as a clear outline of how to do the counting. People unable to serve on a counting team on their assigned Sunday had the responsibility to find someone else on the list to cover for them. Counted money was to be placed in the night deposit at the bank by the counting team immediately after the count. Setting out these clear expectations reassured committee members that they were fulfilling their responsibility as stewards of the congregation's resources. With a clear position description, Betty felt able to ask someone to consider being the offering captain, and with understandable guidelines for counting the offering, Betty found that she was able to encourage new people to sign up as counters.

Sometimes eagerness to get warm bodies to fill a committee outweighs the concern of finding a person who is a good fit for the position. A supervisory relationship includes being clear about the expectations and responsibilities of the position at the same time one nurtures the gifts and learning of the person wishing to fill the position. Ensuring that a person has gifts for the position is every bit as valuable as describing what is involved in the post. For instance, Jill was new to the congregation, having been a member of another congregation before her move to this town and a new teaching position. She wanted to get involved at Cross Street United, but as a teacher she did not want to be typecast by teaching in church school. She wanted something different and so decided to go on the property committee. The chair of this committee, Stanley, was very organized; he liked to let people know what was expected right away, so that everyone knew where he or she stood. When he heard that Jill was interested in becoming a member of the committee, Stanley wanted to get to know her and get a sense of what gifts she brought to this committee. Stanley was happy to take any willing volunteer, but he had learned over the years that to ensure the safety of committee members who enjoy being involved in building projects, he needed to know their skill level.

After some initial conversation, Stanley began by giving Jill the committee's mandate, an outline of the vision of the committee, and a list of its latest projects. Committee membership was for a one-year period with a possibility of renewal for an additional two years. Stanley liked people to make a commitment, yet he was careful not to let people burn out with too many demands on already busy lives. In addition to explaining the mandate, Stanley went over the committee budget and various projects that were ongoing. This routine was followed by an introduction to the work space in the church basement where tools and painting supplies were kept. Stanley was open to hearing how Jill wished to be involved on the committee. Jill really enjoyed painting and had worked as a student painter in her college days. Stanley welcomed her painting ability but also asked her if there was a skill that she would like to learn, something she had not tried before. Jill brightened at this question, as she had always wanted to learn about carpentry but was too nervous to try it on her own. Stanley encouraged her to come out to the work days planned at several points in the church year; he knew he could use her painting skills and was happy to coach her in some beginner's carpentry skills. Not everyone on the property committee was handy with a hammer and paintbrush. On work days, Phillip enjoyed preparing coffee and muffins and a hearty lunch for the work group. Sandra organized work teams, put announcements about work days in the bulletin, and called people with reminders to come and help out. Stanley was creative in getting many people with diverse gifts involved in caring for the church property. Not only did the involvement of many people make lighter work; in addition, individuals felt that they were making a positive contribution to the upkeep of this sacred space.

Aside from conducting work details, the property committee met every other month to review projects in hand, to look ahead at new work, and to evaluate its mandate. Evaluation had two parts. First, Stanley liked to do a regular evaluation of the building to determine what was working well and what new projects needed to take place. Sometimes the committee needed to look at large ventures, like the replacement of the boiler last year. They looked at quotes and made recommendations to the board and oversaw the work in hand. Jill felt excited about working with this group after such a clear introduction to the expectations. A second part of evaluation included looking at how the committee was working and discussing people's learning goals. After being shown how to use some of the carpentry tools, Jill felt enough confidence to sign up for a "Women and Power Tools" workshop run by the local community center.

Failing to explain clearly the expectations and responsibilities when encouraging someone to consider participation on a committee is unhelpful. People will often play down responsibilities, saying, "Just show up to at meetings once a month; there's not much to it," believing that this approach will attract more committee members. However, in my experience, people want to feel that they will make a significant contribution; they appreciate the support that comes from a clearly organized committee mandate and transparent expectations. I really appreciate the insights of Norma deWaal Malefyt, resource development specialist for congregational song, and Howard Vanderwell, resource development specialist for pastoral leadership, at the Calvin Institute of Christian Worship. They both bring years of experience to the area of worship planning and preparation. They raise many questions of worship governance and suggest that two tiers of supervision are necessary: establishing vision and policy, and planning worship. They observe, "A church without clearly established policies for its worship life is like a ship without a rudder, or a traveler without a map."[8] They suggest setting clear roles and responsibilities for those who are going to be involved in worship planning. They offer a sample letter that outlines responsibilities for a new committee member, such as reading the vision statement for worship, worshiping regularly, reading and studying in the area of worship, covenanting to participate fully in planning meetings, and completing all responsibilities in a timely manner. In return, the worship committee makes a commitment to care for committee members by providing continuing education and study materials on worship, organizing productive meetings that include a worship and study component, being clear about assignments, and offering resources needed to complete assignments.

Another aspect of clarifying expectations is outlining the governance structure of the congregation and the committees. The many lines of communication and relationship within a congregation can be confusing for people new to the church. As Matthew discovered as a new member of the worship committee, many relationships are involved in putting together a worship service. In addition to paid staff—the senior pastor, the youth pastor, an intern, and the organist—many groups relate to every worship service. Primary, of course is the worship committee itself. Then there are three choirs: adult, youth, and children's. A subcommittee arranges flowers each

Sunday, as well as seasonal decor coordinated with the liturgical seasons. A subcommittee of greeters not only has responsibility to welcome people, hand out the bulletins, and collect the Sunday offering; its members also review and practice procedures for emergencies such as fire or a worshiper's sudden illness during the service. The church school committee and youth committee need to be involved in worship planning to ensure inclusion of young people in worship and coordination of biblical themes and activities. Office staff members need to be kept in the loop as they develop the bulletin, order regular and seasonal bulletin covers, and coordinate special services such as baptisms, funerals, and weddings.

All of these worship-planning partners are directly accountable to the board, which sets policy and procedure for worship on behalf of the congregation. Malefyt and Vanderwell suggest, "Some policies deal with the logistics and outward practices of worship. . . . But other policies involve theological issues that lie at the very heart of worship."[9] Matthew discovered the supervisory responsibility of the board in regard to worship policies when a member of the congregation asked the worship committee about baptizing her infant granddaughter, Becky, who would be visiting from across the country with her parents, who were not churchgoers. Thinking that requests for baptism are automatically accepted, Matthew learned during discussion at one committee meeting that Cross Street had clear policies for baptisms as set out by the board. In this denomination, baptism acknowledges membership in the faith community, with the congregation offering vows to nurture the child's ongoing spiritual development. Consequently, because Becky's home was at such a distance from Cross Street and her parents had no intention of attending a church in their home location, the board had to refuse the baptism request. The worship committee had the delicate task of suggesting a thanksgiving liturgy to welcome Becky into God's family rather than a baptism that indicated membership. Matthew learned that a congregation is a complex system with many voices contributing to the vision and mission of the church. Being clear about the governance structure of the congregation supports the leadership of those taking on positions of responsibility.

Conflict Resolution Guidelines

Conflict is discussed in more detail in chapter 4, but at this point I want to suggest that conflict or grievance procedures accompany the position description, perhaps in a congregational handbook. Such procedures may seem heavy-handed in a congregation where there may be an assumption of goodwill. However, conflicts do arise, and having a clear process offers guidance at such stressful moments and constitutes part of our call to Christian discipleship. Drawing on his extensive experience in both human resources and faithful church membership, Erwin Berry writes:

> Melding the experience and expertise of the personnel busi-
> ness world with a strong commitment to the nurture and love
> present in the Christian gospel not only "greases the wheels"
> for smooth, efficient staff relationships; it also, in a very real
> way, models the gospel itself. First, it communicates that we care
> enough for the staff and the congregation to set these policies
> in place. Second, it shows that we care enough about the calling
> of the church to model our relationships on those presented to
> us in Scripture.[10]

As part of a covenantal relationship, grievance procedures for both staff and lay leaders need to be spelled out at the beginning of a new relationship, rather than after a conflict has erupted. Such a practice acknowledges our human frailty and the reality that conflict is a normal part of all relationships. Since conflict can range from simple disagreement to a deeper rift, having a procedure with layered responses works well. Denominations may have procedures for dealing with conflict, but the following sample may be adapted.

As mentioned earlier, we are a covenantal people, called by God into community. This call does not mean that we are impervious to the normal day-to-day stresses of being in relationship with one another. We are not "holier than thou." However, God's call to live in covenantal relationship does mean we are called to a standard of behavior that includes respect, clear communication, careful listening to one another, and compassion toward each

Sample Conflict Resolution Procedure

General Principles:

When disagreement arises, all parties are to maintain a respectful attitude toward one another, seeking to find mutual resolution in keeping with God's call to compassionate and just behavior toward our brothers and sisters in Christ. Direct and honest communication between parties in disagreement is preferred as a first step. If disagreement escalates and any party feels unable to work toward resolution, he or she should contact the ministry and personnel committee promptly for support in finding a path to reconciliation. Once informed of the conflict, the ministry and personnel committee will work with all parties to bring resolution. In the event of deeper conflict, the ministry and personnel committee will ensure that all parties to the conflict have opportunity for pastoral care during this stressful period. Timely reconciliation is important if the parties are not to let issues fester and misunderstandings deepen. Therefore, the ministry and personnel committee will move to action within days of being consulted about a conflict.

Procedures

1. When a disagreement arises, parties need to meet face-to-face to discuss the issue for mutual resolution before involving anyone else. Most conflict can be resolved in this mutual encounter. More than one conversation may be helpful.

2. If such meetings are not possible, or if they fail to produce the desired resolution, involving a third party may assist resolution. In the case of a disagreement between paid staff, or an irresolvable disagreement between paid staff and congregation member in a position of responsibility, the third party needs to be a member of the ministry and personnel committee. In the case of disagreement between congregation members in positions of responsibility, a member of the staff or a member of the ministry and personnel committee can be requested.

3. (a) If mutual resolution is not reached between paid staff with the assistance of the ministry and personnel committee, the committee may recommend to the board contracting with a mediator from the denomination (presbytery or conference). Upon recommendation of the mediator, and in the case of irreconcilable conflict, ministry and personnel may recommend to the board a plan of action to resolve the conflict that may include dismissal of one or both of the staff.

(b) In the case of irresolvable disagreement between paid staff and a congregation member in a position of responsibility, the ministry and personnel committee may recommend a plan of action that may require removal of one or both parties from their positions.

(c) In the case of irresolvable conflict between congregation members in positions of responsibility, the ministry and personnel committee may recommend a plan of action that may require removal of one or both parties from their positions of leadership.

other. This behavior is not simply "modeled" by ministry staff and key lay leaders; compassionate and respectful conduct needs to be fully embodied in relationship with one another. Gil Rendle, who brings years of congregational experience both as a pastor and as a congregational consultant, suggests that a board needs to be proactive in establishing a "covenant of leadership" that outlines healthy and appropriate behavior such as respect in speaking with and listening to one another.

> Leaders need to do the hard and necessary up-front work to understand and develop their own spirits, thoughts, and behaviors, which provide the health and the strength that will enable the congregation to live well with the stresses and demands of change. They need to be clear about the behaviors and practices they will need to change within themselves. They need to covenant with one another to make the change happen. Covenanting makes the intention clear and public. To make your intention public is to invite both *support* and *accountability*.[11]

Rendle offers a process for a board to use in developing a "Covenant of Leadership," a covenant that includes promises to God, promises to the congregation, and promises to one another on the board. In addition, Rendle offers suggestions for reinforcing the commitment to live in a covenantal relationship, which include reading the covenant at the beginning of board meetings and regularly evaluating the progress in living the covenant promises.

Conflict is a normal part of all relationships, and congregations are not immune to disagreements; consequently, we need to be clear about how to engage in conflict in healthy ways. Our ways of engaging in conflict and our responses to one another need to demonstrate God's active presence of love and compassion. Being proactive in creating procedures for dealing with conflict and creating a "Covenant of Leadership" are two ways to make expectations transparent.

Covenanting Liturgy

When Bill began his work as senior pastor of Cross Street United Church, a covenanting service celebrated his new relationship with the congregation before God. Traditionally Cross Street did not covenant with other staff aside from the minister. However, Bill felt that a covenant understanding of relationship, in addition to clear contractual arrangements, was an important aspect of a congregation's ministry to its entire staff. Each year Bill suggested a reaffirmation of the covenant relationship with all paid staff as a way of giving visibility to the staff, reminding the members of their responsibilities toward staff, and holding everyone accountable to God in their work together. However, covenants are not solely for paid staff. In thinking about the notion of covenanting with God, the worship committee decided to adopt a yearly liturgy in September at the start of the church-activity year to reaffirm all congregation members' covenantal relationship with God as well as the paid staff. In this service, key lay leaders were named to their positions, children promised to learn about God in church school, youth pledged to bring their energy and innovation to the faith community, members of committees agreed to be accountable to the congregation in their duties, and all members affirmed their ministry outside congregational life. This reaffirmation service provided a great start to the year as people anticipated new programs and spiritual renewal.

Taking time in worship to celebrate the ministry of the whole people of God is a reminder of God's call to each one of us and a tangible way to encourage people to take that call seriously both in congregational commitments and in life outside the church, where people spend most of their time and energy. This celebration provides a base from which to encourage board members and committee members to develop learning covenants as part of their responsibilities of leadership and as part of their growth in Christian discipleship.

In addition to celebrating this ministries liturgy, give thanks throughout the year in worship by making note of particular contributions of individuals and by including the work of the board and committees in the prayers of thanksgiving and intercession. Also, take time at the end of a church year to celebrate the work of members of the congregation, recognizing the devotion and

Sample Covenanting Liturgy

Preparation: If possible, place the baptismal font and a pitcher of water in a prominent location.

Hymn: Choose a hymn that highlights our call to ministry as a covenantal people (for example, "Lord, You Give the Great Commission," "We Have This Ministry," or "I, the Lord of Sea and Sky").[12]

Reminder of God's Call
PRESIDER: We are gathered here in the presence of God to celebrate the ministry to which God has called us each one of us. Young and old; new Christians and cradle Christians; seekers, visionaries, and prophets; social activists, analysts, and gentle listeners—we offer our unique gifts to God and in service to this congregation and the world. *Pour water noisily from pitcher into baptismal font.*
PRESIDER: The water of baptism reminds us of God's grace, invisible yet poured forth in abundance. We celebrate God's gift of grace and our call to share that grace freely with others. Let us covenant with God and one another to our vocation as disciples of Christ.

Responding to God's Call
PRESIDER: Will all board members please stand. *(People will remain standing as each group is called upon.)* Will you fulfill your ministry as members of the board and chairs of congregational committees with commitment and integrity? Will you respect one another's gifts and differences and work together to serve the ministry of Christ and this congregation? Will you respect, trust, and care for the people of this congregation in prayer, word, and action?
RESPONSE: We will, God being our guide.

PRESIDER: Will all ministry staff please stand. *(Pause.)* Will you fulfill your ministry as people chosen by this congregation for particular leadership responsibilities? Will you respect other staff members' gifts and differences, and work together to serve the ministry of Christ and this congregation? Will you respect, trust, and care for the people of this congregation in prayer, word, and action?
RESPONSE: We will, God being our guide.

PRESIDER: Will all committee members please stand. *(Pause.)* Will you fulfill your ministry as members of congregational committees with your unique gifts? Will you respect one another's gifts and differences, and work together to serve the ministry of Christ and this congregation? Will you respect, trust, and care for the people of this congregation in prayer, word, and action?
RESPONSE: We will, God being our guide.

PRESIDER: Will all children and youth please stand. *(Pause.)* Will you fulfill your ministry as members of this congregation, participating in church school, choirs, youth group, *(name other groups)*, worship, and community gatherings with energetic commitment? Will you respect one another's gifts and differences, and work together to serve the ministry of Christ and this congregation? Will you respect, trust, and care for the people of this congregation in prayer, word, and action?
RESPONSE: We will, God being our guide.

PRESIDER: Will all church members please stand. *(Pause.)* Will you fulfill your ministry as ones called by God to share love and compassion in the world? Will you respect one another's gifts and differences, and work together to serve the ministry of Christ in the world? Will you respect, trust, and care for people locally and globally in prayer, word, and action?
RESPONSE: We will, God being our guide.

Affirmation of Faith
PRESIDER: Still standing, let us join together in reaffirming our faith in the reading of *(a denominational creed, congregational mission statement, or other covenantal statement)*.

Blessing
ALL: We are filled with the gift of God's grace and authorized to minister in God's name through our baptism. In all our words and actions, may God bless us and keep us, may God's face shine upon us, be gracious toward us, and give us peace. Amen.

Hymn: Choose a hymn that highlights our call to ministry as a covenantal people, such as one of those mentioned above.

commitment people bring to their faith and their ministry. Make note of those who are stepping down from positions of responsibility. If the budget allows, offer a tangible thank-you in the form of gift certificate for a Christian bookstore, or a lapel pin with a religious symbol. One congregation had boxes of gift cards printed with a simple pen-and-ink sketch of the church building to give out as thank-you gifts

A congregation can live its call to ministry by creating an encouraging learning environment in which staff and members can deepen their faith and nurture their leadership gifts. Transparent expectations of role and responsibility can be offered through a position description and congregational procedures for conflict resolution. A commitment to learning can be supported through development of learning goals that form the focus of supervisory conversations. And all the ministries of the people of God can be supported and blessed through intentional actions such as a covenanting liturgy during worship.

SEVEN

FEEDBACK, REFLECTION, EVALUATION, AND CLOSURE

To engage in transformative learning, both supervisor and supervisee need to take time for reflection to integrate what has been learned about new ways of thinking, feeling, and acting. Part of the reflective process can include seeking feedback from others to broaden our perspectives, to help us see ourselves as others see us, and to receive constructive suggestions. In addition, evaluation provides a time to review, gather insights, and perhaps renew, reevaluate, or reform learning directions. While learning is a continual lifelong process, specific learning goals are time-limited, thus benefiting from celebration and closure, a time of thanksgiving for new growth in leadership formation, and closure of the particular project or topic being explored.

Hearing, Receiving, and Acting on Feedback

Since part of the learning process can include hearing, receiving, and acting on feedback, I encourage supervisees actively to seek and reflect upon feedback. In general, feedback is information about our ways of speaking, acting, and being, as perceived by others. Specifically, feedback is related to learning goals developed by the supervisee.

Feedback can be explicit and implicit. For instance, explicit feedback might be a comment offered to a facilitator after a "visioning" workshop: "I really found that your clear leadership guided the group to develop a useful vision for the congregation." At times explicit feedback may not be possible, as during a pastoral visit. Asking for feedback while visiting a family in grief is not appropriate, yet feedback may be implied in the way family members respond to the visitor. Sharing feelings, shedding tears, and recounting stories about the deceased are implicit indications that the pastoral visitor created a safe and inviting environment for conversation.

For feedback to be most useful it needs to have three strands: hearing, receiving, and acting. Once we hear feedback from others, we need time to reflect on what we have heard. Perhaps the feedback offered is useful, perhaps not. We may decide to reject what we have heard, or we may decide to receive this information as part of our learning about ourselves. After receiving this information, we can integrate it into our way of being and act on it. Learning how to hear, receive, and act on the feedback offered helps us to gain greater self-awareness and deeper insights about ourselves.

Feedback is an important facet of congregational life, where we are living in a community with diverse perspectives. Feedback from the generous and constructive contributions of those who come into contact with our leadership firsthand offers us an opportunity to be enriched by the gifts and experience of others, to grow as leaders. Adult educator Patricia Cranton writes, "One of the few undisputed principles of learning is that learning is facilitated by regular, ongoing feedback; this is as true for transformative learning as for the simple acquisition of knowledge and skills."[1] Whatever learning goals are formulated, whether a concrete task or project, an idea to explore, or new skills to develop, feedback can be a useful element in our journey of transformative learning. Seeking feedback can be as simple as bouncing ideas around with someone who has more experience, inviting comments on a written reflection or journal, or developing a survey asking specific questions about our work.

The process of hearing, receiving, and acting on feedback requires a deliberate approach. Not all feedback is useful or constructive. For feedback to be helpful, it needs to be timely, constructive, intentional, and requested.

Helpful Feedback Is Timely

Choosing the right time to offer feedback can affect how a person will receive this information and make the feedback more useful. As a minister leading worship each Sunday, Bill has found that directly after a worship service, he is not receptive to critical feedback. He is too close to the event, too invested in the preparation, and personally vulnerable from presiding at worship. However, he does enjoy a good discussion with congregation members later in the week about how they experienced the Sunday service. From time to time, he has arranged "talk-back" sessions on a Monday evening to hear from congregation members about their thoughts on worship at Cross Street United Church. At those sessions, people have offered great suggestions for future services, affirmation of Bill's worship leadership, and gentle critiques of what they felt went well and what did not go well.

On the other hand, Phyllis, chair of Christian education, experienced a time when feedback given too long after an event was unhelpful. She recalled a school principal giving her feedback directly before a school assembly: "I hope you are not going to use a slide-show approach in this assembly. That approach did not work very well last year." Both the proximity of this negative feedback to a new activity and the distance from the last event made this feedback both hurtful and useless. Constructive feedback about the previous assembly within a few weeks of the actual event would have given Phyllis time to think about what she had done and how she could do it differently in the future.

Helpful Feedback Is Constructive

Offering helpful feedback may take a little effort. Simply saying, "I really liked what you did" doesn't give the recipient any clues about what impressed you. Conversely, saying, "I didn't really enjoy that presentation" doesn't help the presenter to consider ways to change or improve the work. For maximum impact, feedback needs to be constructive, meaning that it should offer encouragement as well as a clear and specific critique. Charlotte, a new member of the lay readers' team, had created a learning goal of becoming more involved in leading worship, so she had volunteered to read Scripture. She had attended the training session and was reading Scripture in the service for the first time on Sunday. To get a sense of how she came across to the congregation, she asked Deirdre to give her feedback after the service. In thinking about what she would say to Charlotte, Deirdre wanted to offer positive comments along with a specific critique but, overall, to be as encouraging as possible. To be constructive, Deirdre wanted to describe what she had observed and experienced, as well as to suggest what Charlotte could do next time. After the service Deirdre said, "When you read the text, you enunciated clearly and read with a measured pace, so I was able to hear very well. In your reading, you conveyed the meaning behind the words. You really wanted the listeners to understand what they were hearing. Perhaps when you read next time, you could be less attached to the written word and look up from the Bible to make more eye contact with the congregation. That way you will be more welcoming, and the warmth of your personality will come from beyond the lectern." Charlotte appreciated Deirdre's clear descriptions and observations and felt she had explicit information from which to make changes. Deirdre even offered to listen to her practice next week in the sanctuary, if she didn't mind having three noisy children running through the pews. Charlotte laughed and said she thought this would give her good practice in trying to project above the background noise that often occurred during a worship service.

In giving feedback, it is often helpful to name a person's gifts and the things she did well along with suggested areas for improvement. One note of caution is not to fall into the formula, "You were great . . . but." People wait for the "but" and end up not truly hearing the positive comments. Deidre was able to be as clear and specific about her positive comments as she was about her critique.

Another dimension of what makes feedback constructive is offering a critique that can be acted upon. Phyllis remembered a teacher evaluation early in her career when she was told, "If only you were a little taller, you would offer a better presence to the class."

Phyllis remarked that since she could not do anything about her height of five feet, she found this comment to be utterly useless. However, what was implied in the feedback and what she did take to heart was the notion that she could improve her sense of presence in the classroom by seeking wisdom from more experienced teachers. In their comments, she was offered many useful, specific, and constructive suggestions.

Helpful Feedback Is Intentional

Seeking feedback takes courage, because we put our egos on the line and may feel vulnerable to criticism. Seeking feedback means inviting thoughts and comments from others and soliciting ideas and constructive suggestions. When Frank and Astrid became co-chairs of the new members committee, their learning goal was to come up with interesting ideas for welcoming new people to Cross Street United. Before generating any ideas, they wanted to get a sense of how welcome people felt when they entered the doors of the church building for the first time. They developed a feedback sheet asking why newcomers had decided to come to Cross Street; what their impressions of the building and worship service were; whether they had easily found the restrooms, nursery facilities, bulletins, and hymnbooks they needed; whether they had attended coffee time after worship; and whether people had made them feel welcome. Frank put the feedback sheets, pencils, and a box for responses in the entrance to the sanctuary, so people could respond anonymously. As people arrived, they were given a feedback sheet and a pencil along with the bulletin, and were asked to fill in their comments after the service.

After reading feedback sheets over a period of months, Frank and Astrid realized that they had their work cut out for them. Although people were attracted to the historic building, they did not feel welcomed by members of the congregation. Astrid had been a churchgoer all her life, and she learned that most people coming to Cross Street for the first time were completely new to any church experience whatsoever. Consequently, Astrid had to change her assumptions about what visitors needed when they entered the building. Newcomers needed basic explanations about how to participate in worship, information about the congregation, and directions for finding locations in the building. Responses to the feedback sheet included suggestions. One person proposed offering tours of the building for visitor orientation. Another recommended escorting visitors to a place to sit during worship and showing families where their children would go during church school.

One response that surprised Astrid was a request to have the Lord's Prayer written out in full, rather than just the title of the prayer listed in the bulletin. As someone new to church, this visitor did not know the words. Although Astrid's assumptions about what people needed as they entered Cross Street were being turned upside down, she was nonetheless delighted with all the responses and grateful that people had taken time to offer suggestions. She also wondered about inviting a few of the newer members of the congregation to be part of the new members committee to bring their fresh perspectives to the committee's goal of improving the welcome of visitors and hoped-for members. Frank was pleased that deliberately seeking feedback had offered such rich learning. Frank and Astrid offered a report on their learning to the board, thus being accountable for their learning as well as sharing their insights with others.

Helpful Feedback Is Requested

Feedback is easier to hear when it has been requested than when it is offered as unsolicited advice, and easier to hear when we are able to negotiate how and when we like to receive feedback. Over his years as a pastor, Bill has gone out of his way to ask for feedback, thus creating an open environment in which people feel free to offer their thoughts. However, Bill has been clear about how he likes to receive feedback. As mentioned earlier, Bill knows his sensitivity to hearing comments immediately following worship. So when someone wants to launch into a critique of his sermon at coffee time after the service, Bill gently asks if they can meet later in the week when he is able to give the conversation his full attention. He requests a time that will make him more receptive to hearing comments. Also, Bill knows that he does not like to be yelled at. He understands that people offer comments in the heat of the moment, but he knows his receptivity to criticism offered in a loud voice is poor. Again, Bill requests another time to have conversation when the person may be cooler and calmer.

Knowing that giving and receiving feedback can be difficult, the ministry and personnel committee has created structures to encourage greater receptivity to feedback. First, Gus, as chair of the ministry and personnel committee, asks each staff person to choose a liaison from the committee. The liaison meets regularly with the staff person for conversation about his or her work, both celebrations and frustrations. The function of the liaison is to be a bridge between the staff and the committee, to offer support and critique to the staff member, and to be an advocate for him or her at committee meetings. Staff members have appreciated this structure. In addition, at annual review time, Gus and committee members meet with committees relevant to particular staff positions to request feedback. For instance, Gus meets with the worship committee and pastoral care committee to request feedback on Bill's leadership and to ask how the committee's work is going. Through this structure, the ministry and personnel committee is more organized about requesting and offering feedback.

A Word of Caution

Although feedback is useful in our learning process, we must not be naive about people's motivations in giving feedback. Sometimes wounded and negative people offer their anger and personal issues disguised as well-meaning feedback. Bill has learned to hold all comments at a safe distance while he takes time to think about what he is hearing, to evaluate both the comment and the critic. One event that stands out in his mind is from his experience as a young pastor in his first congregation. One Monday morning, a very angry woman appeared in his office, supposedly to offer her feedback about Bill's sermon. Bill felt as though she was tearing his sermon to shreds. He was devastated. The comments undermined his confidence and ate away at his sense of call. He brooded alone for several months. Finally he talked to a trusted member of the board, Maggie, about his concern that perhaps he was not a fit pastor for this congregation. As Maggie listened, the story of his encounter with this angry individual came spilling out. After listening quietly to his concerns, Maggie offered two pieces of counsel. "Bill, have you considered that this person's comments are not about you?" She went on to relate the sad and tortured life of this woman, who never lost an opportunity to pour vitriol on anyone in her path as a way of easing her own pain. "The angry comments were about her personal issues, not about your sermon," Maggie assured him. Bill learned not to take comments so personally.

Her second piece of advice was to "check it out." Maggie suggested that when we hear feedback that upsets our preconceived notions of ourselves and our abilities, we should, before jumping off the deep end into abject despair and self-doubt, check it out with other people, trusted individuals who can give clear and honest responses. When we hear the same feedback from a number of trusted people, then it is time to take the constructive critique seriously.

Reflecting on Our Learning

Taking time for reflection enhances our learning by creating space for review—to see where we started on our journey, how far we have come, and where we want to go next. Reflection allows us to note changes in our thinking, feeling, and acting as a result of our learning. We may achieve new insights, discover another direction for our learning, wrestle with challenges, and feel a sense of satisfaction in what we have accomplished so far. The following samples offer tools for reflection. The first example, "Reflecting on our Learning," is a simple exercise for a quick weekly review. The second example, "Deepening our Learning through Reflection" is a more in-depth reflection that might be used for a presentation to a group or to a supervisor when the learning is well on the way. These tools are useful in any kind of reflection on learning, whether in formal supervision with a field-education student or intern, or in a less formal relationship with a committee chair or member.

The first example, "Reflecting on Our Learning," may be used as a template for ongoing reflection, as a way to review your learning goals, perhaps in preparation for an upcoming supervisory conversation.

Reflecting on Our Learning

As you think about your learning goal, use the following questions for reflection:

1. What one event related to your learning goal stands out for you this week?
2. What's happened in your learning so far?
3. How do you feel about it?
4. What are you learning?
5. What might you do differently as you continue your learning?
6. What questions or issues have arisen?
7. What questions or issues would you like to discuss with your supervisor?

This second reflection process, a more in-depth tool, might be used for a more complex issue arising from the learning goals. Added to this template is a section on "Preparing for a Presentation," intended to focus reflection on presenting the chosen experience to a supervisor or group. A supervisor may be the minister or a committee chair. A group may be a committee. For instance, a person on the Christian education committee may use this template in preparing a presentation on a learning goal related to the work of the Christian education committee.

Deepening Our Learning through Reflection

Name the Experience

Choose an event, a moment, a conversation, or a situation to reflect on. As you recall the event, ask yourself:

- What happened?
- Who was involved?
- What did you do or say?

Explore the Experience

To explore another layer in this event, ask yourself:

- How did you feel?
- What challenged, stimulated, or disturbed you?
- How did others react in the situation?

Dig Deeper

To expand your thinking, ask yourself:

- What do you think about the situation?
- What core values emerge for you and others as you think about this event?
- What values that others hold are different from your own?
- What social issues, power issues, or economic issues are at work?

Make Faith Connections

To find God at work in this event, ask yourself:

- Where is God present for you in this situation?
- Where is God present for others?
- Does this event remind you of a Scripture passage, a hymn, or other resources from your faith tradition?
- What theological issues or themes are present?

- What traditions of our congregation and the denomination speak to this situation?
- In what ways are you affirmed or challenged in your present actions or beliefs?

Learn

To name your discoveries, ask yourself:

- What questions still linger?
- In what ways were you challenged to change present actions or beliefs?
- What have you learned about yourself?
- What you have learned about others?
- What have you learned about God?
- What do you need?
- What will you do now?

Pray

To conclude your reflection, take time with God and write a prayer emerging from this event.

Preparing for Presentation

As you think about discussing your learning with others, such as your supervisor or committee, think about how you would like the group to focus. Discussion is not problem solving but a way to deepen your personal reflection. Here are some questions to focus your preparation to present to your supervisor or group:

- Is there a question still lingering on which you would like to solicit the wisdom of others?
- Do you want to hear what others have experienced in similar situations?
- Do you want to hear thoughts about further theological or biblical connections?
- Do you want to know where others see God at work?

Theological students, whether in field education or in an internship, may find this reflection process a useful framework when presenting to their supervisor, a congregational reflection group (as adopted by some denominations and seminaries), or a seminary class. In a less formal setting in a congregation, this reflection process may be useful in looking back on a complex experience involving a number of factors to sort through. Personal reflection is always helpful in drawing out the threads of an event and naming the discoveries. More helpful is an opportunity to reflect with others, whether in a one-on-one supervisory conversation or with a committee covenanted to work on particular learning goals. Seeking wisdom, experience, and further theological insights will broaden perspectives and deepen learning.

Evaluating Our Learning

Basically, evaluation asks individuals and groups, "What have you learned from this experience?" To identify what has been learned within the supervisory period named on the learning covenant, evaluation looks back at initial hopes as outlined in the learning goals and identifies steps along the learning journey and the point which people have reached. The object of this process is not to find fault or to assign blame if things did not turn out as expected. The intent is to discover what went well and what might be done differently for future learning.

In the context of a learning covenant, evaluation is not designed to test people on the content of their learning. Evaluation encourages people to name the insights from their learning and to explore how this learning has shaped them as people of faith and as leaders. As mentioned in chapter 3, educator Jane Vella suggests three layers of reflection that I believe are useful: content, process, and premise. *Content reflection* asks, "What have I learned?" thus inviting the learner to look at the information and insights gleaned. *Process reflection* asks, "How have I learned?" as a way to consider how learning took place, what elements or people contributed to that learning. And *premise reflection* looks at the underlying meaning of the learning for the supervisee by asking, "Why does this learning matter to me, to others, or to God?"

In the supervisory relationship, offering thoughts, insights, and feedback as time and opportunity present themselves is important in the learning relationship. Saving up feedback until the end of the learning experience does not allow time for the learner to try different styles, skills, or methods. Offering feedback along the way is preferable, with ongoing opportunities to evaluate learning, and with a final evaluation intended as a summing-up of the whole experience. There must be no surprises in the final evaluation. In a relationship of trust and honesty, all participants are able to be frank and open in what they need to say. Evaluation is a summative process that includes working at the learning goals, gathering feedback, and reflecting regularly on learning.

Evaluation is not a word that crops up much in congregational ministry. Lots of people agree to take on tasks in the church without the prospect, welcome or otherwise, of being evaluated. Yet when done well, evaluation is an affirming and transforming process. However, evaluation needs to be initiated with care because many people have memories of school days when evaluation undermined self-worth. Adult educator Pierre Dominice notes:

> For many adults the school grading system has nourished their doubts about themselves. Grades are very often taken as more than an indicator of what has been learned. Grades and diplomas earned during their school years seem to give adults their identities as learners. . . . Adults who were mediocre students have continuing doubts about their capacity to learn unless they obtain better grades in their adult learning.[2]

To dispel previous negative experiences, evaluation in a congregational setting can be a time for a learner to identify discoveries and to grow in faith and ability as a leader through self-evaluation. Evaluative input from a supervisor can reinforce the positive aspects of learning and build up the confidence of a learner for future endeavors. As noted before, learning is an ongoing as well as a summative process that includes celebrating accomplishments and naming new vistas of learning. Sometimes evaluation can be difficult when intended learning goes astray, so compassion is an important ingredient in evaluation. People

begin with the greatest of intentions, but sometimes life inter-
venes to set a person off course. Developing and implementing
a learning covenant takes time, energy, and commitment; therefore, acknowledging the valuable contribution of this learning to
an individual's vocational formation, and to the congregation's
ministry as a whole, is important.

For evaluation to be most effective, an evaluation process and
questions can be established right at the beginning of a learning
relationship; thus everyone knows that the learning journey will
include ongoing, midpoint and end-point summative exercises and
knows how those exercises will look. Even though each person's
learning goals will be different, wise leaders will use a standard evaluation form such as the one offered below to convey that evaluation
is a normal part of the learning process for the whole community.
The evaluation questions are meant to be a jumping-off point for
an evaluative conversation in supervision; they can be adapted by
learners as they evaluate their learning. Establishing the evaluative process may include being clear about when, how, and with
whom the evaluation will take place. Evaluation can take place in
regular supervisory conversations, at a midpoint in the learning to
see how people are doing, and at the end of the learning journey
to sum up the whole experience. Evaluation is part of the ongoing
supervisory relationship, whether with an individual supervisor or a
committee. If evaluations are to be written, stating clearly what will
happen to the paperwork will offer further clarity in the process.
I believe that the evaluation belongs to the learner, and that there
is no need for the supervisor to keep a copy for his or her files.

Bringing Closure to Our Learning Relationships

Within all relationships, whether one-on-one or in groups, there is
a beginning and an ending, an entry point and a conclusion. Even
if a committee continues for many years, each year brings its own
completion of hopes, tasks, and learning goals. Also, in the natural
life of any committee, some people will finish their terms of appointment, and new members will be welcomed in the upcoming

Sample Evaluation Tool

As you think back over the creation, ongoing progress, and implementation of your learning goal, use the following questions, or those pertinent to the learning situation, to evaluate your learning.

- What feelings best describe your experience?
- In what ways have you worked to achieve your learning goal?
- What progress have you made?
- What insights have emerged?
- How has your learning contributed to your sense of vocation as one called by God to serve the church and the world?
- What have you learned about the areas of ministry in which you do well?
- What have you learned about aspects of your ministry that need strengthening?
- What significant relationships have you developed?
- In what ways has the supervisor been helpful or unhelpful to your learning?
- What new insights and skills have you been able to incorporate thus far?

Other comments:

church year. In the one-on-one supervisory relationship, the term of the learning covenant concludes, and there is need for closure of the learning relationship. The learning covenant may be renewed for another year, but drawing this particular covenant to a close is part of the summing up and evaluation of the learning; it offers an opportunity to go in new learning directions, perhaps with a new supervisor. Closure functions as bridge between two situations—the ending of one relationship and the beginning of another. Closure also functions as an evaluation of the learning partners' relationship, whether a committee or a duo. What follows is a process for closure used for many years in the theological field-education program at Emmanuel College, Toronto, here adapted for use in congregations.

Healthy Closure in a Supervisory Relationship

To begin the process of closure, supervisor and supervisee might talk about what the supervisory relationship has meant in the learning process, recounting the relationship's history and acknowledging good times and bad. A committee can also talk together about the learning relationship experienced throughout the year. The following questions, handed out ahead of a final meeting, may prompt conversation about the experience:

- What are the important things to remember and celebrate?
- What regrets or disappointments need to be shared?
- What things are left unfinished?
- How might things have been done differently?
- How do we feel about saying good-bye?
- What other experiences of saying good-bye come to mind?
- What images, symbols, metaphors, or stories could be used to describe our relationship?
- What would we like to share with each other about our future directions or plans?
- What kind of ritual or symbolic action will best enable us to say good-bye?
- What would we like to give to each other as a reminder of this experience?
- What does saying good-bye mean from a faith perspective?

One aspect of closure is letting go. This step involves realizing that we become an individual separate from the group, separate from the supervisory relationship, letting go of group values and norms and moving to individual values and norms, nonetheless enriched by the experience. What can be a challenge is resisting the temptation to cling to the relationships. Taking time to talk about the relationship and say good-bye to this particular configuration is one way to let go. Sometimes letting go is a real leave-taking, when a field-education student or intern will leave the congregation and return to the seminary for continued studies or go to another pastoral charge as a newly ordained minister. Within a congregation, people are not necessarily leaving the context, but they may decide to take a break from an informal learning covenant, to change committees, to step down from chairing a committee, or to work with another supervisor for a different learning experience. Letting go means changing the supervisory relationship to embrace new possibilities.

And finally, taking time to celebrate the life of the group is an important aspect of bringing closure to a learning relationship. Celebrate with food and ritual, with words and blessings for the journey. Without proper closure, we are likely to be left with emotional "loose ends" that complicate our lives unnecessarily and prevent us from moving on. There is a need for closure of our learning journey through the evaluation process, and there is also a need for closure at the relational level.

Through his many years as a supervisor, Bill had enjoyed the varied learning relationships with field-education students and interns. In his experience, a final evaluation was a gathering of all the best learning through all the highs and lows of ministry for both himself and the supervisee. In addition, Bill and the supervisee were able to consider future directions in their ministry leadership through specific critical reflection that was encouraging and challenging. Bill had reveled in the accomplishments in his learning as well as the challenges, and he hoped that each supervisee left his congregations with the same feeling. The icing on the cake was a time for celebration that recognized the completion of the learning covenant in a final Sunday worship service, followed by a celebratory lunch.

In less formal relationships within the congregation, taking time for feedback, reflection, evaluation, and closure is equally as important. Feedback offers perceptions from others that may broaden learning. Self-reflection and reflection with others deepen learning; evaluation acknowledges both the learning and the learning relationship; and closure brings completion to a fruitful learning experience. Frank and Astrid experienced the flow of this learning process when they began by setting a learning goal of coming up with interesting ideas for welcoming new people to Cross Street United Church. They had no idea where their learning would take them. They found explicit feedback from visitors most helpful in challenging their assumptions: congregation members were not as welcoming as they assumed, and visitors often had little church experience. Frank and Astrid enjoyed times for reflection on their learning with the new members committee, where wisdom was shared and great ideas were generated. Further reflection was offered by the board following a theological reflection presentation by Frank and Astrid as a summative report on all the feedback sheets they had received. Evaluation helped Frank and Astrid to acknowledge both the point at which their learning began and all the discoveries they had made along the way; it also enabled them to notice how valuable the members of their committee were in the reflection and learning process. At the end of the year, all committee members took time for closure, as some members were leaving the committee because their terms had come to an end, and brand-new members were joining in the fall. As in all good endings, there was a time for prayer and a time for feasting, as committee members gave thanks to one another and to God, and shared in a potluck supper together, celebrating their relationships and their rich learning throughout the year.

Learning is not an easy process; it requires courage to engage with others in hearing, receiving, and acting on feedback—sometimes feedback filled with praise, at other times feedback that offers challenge. Critical reflection on our learning presents an opportunity for transformation as our previous ways of thinking, feeling, and acting are examined and renewed. Learning is a lifelong journey of discovery that embraces our whole self, stretching us in anticipated and serendipitous ways. And taking time to celebrate the growth and the growth pains in community reflection, thanksgiving, and feasting is one of the distinct joys of congregational life.

EIGHT

SPIRITUALITY AND SUPERVISION

At the heart of supervision is the learning relationship between supervisor and supervisee, an opportunity for mutual learning in which the intended purposes are vocational formation for leadership within the congregation and an individual's personal and faith development. A primary assumption is that this learning is a spiritual journey.

This spiritual journey has two aspects—the development of spirituality *first* within the learner, and *second* within the learning process itself. *Spirituality,* a much-used term, tends to have great meaning for some but sounds akin to a new-age abandonment of Christian principles for others. Adult educator Linda J. Vogel, professor of Christian education at Garrett-Evangelical Theological Seminary in Evanston, Illinois, and deacon in the United Methodist Church, addresses the concept of spirituality in the learning of adults, observing:

> Defining *spirituality* is a nebulous task; there is no commonly agreed-upon definition. Some find the term to their liking; others find it too vague and without substance. Some feel that the word spirituality diminishes their religious faith, whatever it might be; for others it is a preferred term precisely because it does not contain particular doctrinal, historical, or theological content.[1]

Rather than defining particular theologies, denominations, or even faiths, *spirituality* describes the way learning and the learner are fully embraced by God's grace and love. And conversely, the learner and the learning can be focused on developing a deeper and closer relationship with God.

When a learner develops learning goals within the framework of leadership formation for congregational ministry, he or she has an opportunity to deepen faith and to reflect theologically. For instance, when a supervisor and supervisee individually and together pray regularly about congregational concerns and hopes for learning, naming struggles and offering thanks for insights, they both grow in their facility for prayer as conversation with God. Prayer often becomes neglected in a busy congregation. I learned tremendous wisdom from a board chair, Celia, who discerned that rather than pushing a decision through when all were tired or confused, unclear about their feelings, or lashing out inappropriately, it was more prudent for her to ask the board to take more time for reflection, contemplation, conversation, and prayer. Rarely does a decision need to be made immediately, although as anxiety increases, the desire to make a decision usually becomes more urgent. At times Celia would intervene in a discussion and suggest that we needed more time to think and pray about this decision. After a prayerful month, we often came back to the decision at the next meeting with more clarity and wisdom, and certainly more patience. All learning in a congregation is framed by our relationships with one another as stemming from a foundation of God's delight in the learner as child of God and as disciple in Christ's ministry.

In addition, a learner, whether supervisor or supervisee, needs to be encouraged to practice other spiritual disciplines—regular worship attendance, biblical reading, fasting, confession, hospitality, social-justice advocacy, and so on. Many resources are available to encourage exploration and incorporation of spiritual disciplines in the learning goals, and I highly recommend creating a library of such resources for supervisees, supervisors, and congregations.

I strongly believe that learning itself is a deeply spiritual enterprise. Adult educators working in nonreligious settings acknowledge the spirituality of learning. Jane Vella, respected adult educator, has coined the term "spirited epistemology" to describe the work of education and learning. Epistemology is "the study of knowing and the art of learning," and her use of "spirited" comes from Augustine's notion that no one can teach another person anything. All we can do is to prepare the way for the work of the Holy Spirit.[2] Within her concept of spirited epistemology, Vella offers several assumptions. First, the learner is honored as fully the agent in his or her learning. Rather than being considered objects of teaching, as passive receptacles for a teacher's wisdom, learners are full participants and decision makers in their lives and in their learning. Second, every moment is an opportunity for learning— and thus for greater spiritual development through self-awareness, and a deeper understanding of and compassion toward others. And third, when we reflect on our learning, examining our assumptions and embracing new ways of being, we are engaged in a process of transformation. In this sense, transformative learning is *metanoia,* a spiritual conversion, a reorientation of one's life toward God.

I believe that in a congregational setting a learning relationship between supervisor and supervisee is spiritual, one that assumes the presence of God. God is the third partner in the learning dialogue, the guiding principle for all conversation, and the spirit that invites us to fulfill our greatest potential. The core of the learning relationship is dialogue in which supervisor and supervisee approach one another with respect and excitement for what may unfold in their work together. Each is accountable to the other to be fully present in the learning, as an attentive listener, a strong advocate, and a gentle challenger.

Vogel asserts that learning is holistic, because it includes examining beliefs and ways of being that are destructive, becoming open and accepting of others, and finding life-giving ways of relating to self and others. Holistic learning includes attention to creating a hospitable space in a congregation where substantial learning dialogue can take place. According to Vogel:

> When we are committed to safe and hospitable space where true dialogue can occur, it becomes possible to engage even the most controversial issues in ways that are respectful. Adults can learn to agree to disagree in respectful ways that do not attack the value or integrity of others whose deeply held values may be different.[3]

As outlined in earlier chapters, creating a hospitable space includes not only the fun-filled experiences of potluck suppers and chats over refreshments following worship. Hospitality includes all our ways of gathering, and also involves creating policies and procedures for establishing right relations with staff, addressing sexual abuse, managing conflict, and so on. Hospitality means creating an environment of safety for the most vulnerable in our midst.

Reviewing all our efforts to create a holistic environment for transformative learning, how will we identify the fruits of that spirited epistemology? Leona M. English, assistant professor of adult education at Saint Francis Xavier University in Nova Scotia, suggests that authentic spiritual development includes three components: (1) a strong sense of self; (2) care, concern, and outreach to others; and (3) continuous attention to self-reflection and theological reflection as a way to examine our assumptions and grow in faith. As mentioned earlier, learning takes courage and requires a sense of self-esteem. Growth in self-worth and the adoption of healthy approaches to life and living demonstrate one element of spiritual development. Care for others is another dimension:

> A fully integrated spiritual person reaches beyond his or her self and acknowledges the interdependence of all of creation, appreciates the uniqueness of others, and ultimately assumes responsibility for caring and being concerned about other humans and the natural order.[4]

Reaching beyond ourselves characterizes spiritual maturity and is part of our call from God to care for others. As people of faith, we acknowledge a power greater than ourselves, a spirit of compassion for all creation that we attempt to embrace and emulate. Self-reflection and theological reflection offer ways to consider what we do, what we think, and what we believe, and thus move us toward becoming more mature, compassionate, and faithful co-creators with God.

NOTES

Chapter 2

1. Peter Vaill, *Learning as a Way of Being: Strategies for Survival in a World of Permanent White Water* (San Francisco: Jossey-Bass, 1996).
2. Thomas R. Hawkins, *The Learning Congregation: A New Vision of Leadership* (Louisville: Westminster John Knox, 1997), 3.
3. Jim Herrington, R. Robert Creech, and Trisha Taylor, *The Leader's Journey: Accepting the Call to Personal and Congregational Transformation* (San Francisco: Jossey-Bass, 2003), 6.
4. *Congregation Organization Handbook,* prepared by Support to Local Ministries Unit, General Council Office (Toronto: United Church of Canada, 2006).
5. Herrington et al., *The Leader's Journey,* 18.
6. Ibid., 33.
7. Ibid., 35.
8. Ibid., 44.
9. Ibid., 45–46.
10. Ibid., 36.
11. Ibid., 64–65.
12. This exercise is adapted from Dennis Linn, Sheila Fabricant, and Matthew Linn, *Sleeping with Bread: Holding What Gives You Life* (New York: Paulist Press, 2002).
13. For an outline of this process of theological reflection in small groups and supervisory sessions, please refer to Abigail Johnson, *Reflecting with God: Connecting Faith and Daily Life in Small Groups* (Herndon, Va.: Alban Institute, 2004).

Chapter 3

1. Jane Vella, *Learning to Listen, Learning to Teach: The Power of Dialogue in Educating Adults* (San Francisco: Jossey-Bass, 2002), 10.
2. Paul Tournier, *The Meaning of Person* (New York: Harper & Row, 1971), 17.
3. Patricia Cranton, *Understanding and Promoting Transformative Learning: A Guide for Educators of Adults* (San Francisco: Jossey-Bass, 1994), 4.
4. Ibid., 10.
5. Ibid., 12.
6. Ibid., 16.
7. Ibid., 17.
8. Ibid., 18.
9. Ibid., 26.
10. Ibid., 72.
11. Ibid., 166.
12. Pierre Domincé, *Learning from Our Lives* (San Francisco: Jossey-Bass, 2000).
13. Ibid., xv.
14. Ibid., 6.
15. Ibid., 8.
16. Ibid., 10
17. Ibid., 16.
18. Ibid., 20.
19. Ibid., 25.
20. Wilma Fraser, *Learning From Experience: Empowerment or Incorporation?* (Leicester, Great Britain: National Institute of Adult Continuing Education, 1996), 42.

Chapter 4

1. Roy Pneuman, "Nine Common Sources of Conflict in Congregations" in David B. Lott, ed., *Conflict Management in Congregations* (Herndon, Va.: Alban Institute, 2001), 51.
2. Denise W. Goodman, *Congregational Fitness: Healthy Practices for Layfolk* (Herndon, Va.: Alban Institute, 2000), 6.
3. Ibid., 6.
4. Speed B. Leas, "When Conflict Erupts in Your Church" in Lott, *Conflict Management in Congregations,* 8.
5. Ibid., 16.

6. James A. Sparks, "When Criticism Comes: Understanding and Working through Our Defensiveness" in Lott, *Conflict Management in Congregations*, 95.
7. Edwin Friedman, *Generation to Generation: Family Process in Church and Synagogue* (New York: Guilford Press, 1985), 35.
8. Such problem-solving approaches can be found in books such as Christopher Moore, *The Mediation Approach: Practical Strategies for Resolving Conflict* (San Francisco: Jossey-Bass, 1996); and Roger Fisher and William Ury, *Getting to Yes: Negotiating Agreement Without Giving In* (Boston: Houghton Mifflin, 1981).
9. John Winslade and Gerald Monk, *Narrative Mediation: A New Approach to Conflict Resolution* (San Francisco: Jossey Bass, 2000), xi.
10. Ibid., 3.
11. Ibid., 3.
12. Ibid., 44.
13. Ibid., 69.

Chapter 5

1. Patricia Cranton, *Understanding and Promoting Transformative Learning: A Guide for Educators of Adults* (San Francisco: Jossey-Bass, 1994), 131.
2. Ibid., 130.
3. Ibid., 73.
4. Winslade and Monk, *Narrative Mediation*, 50.
5. Ibid., 117.
6. Janet O. Hagberg, "Sharing Power as an Expression of Faith" in Robert Banks and Kimberly Powell, eds., *Faith in Leadership: How Leaders Live Out Their Faith in Their Work—and Why It Matters* (San Francisco: Jossey-Bass, 2000), 97.
7. Ibid., 98.
8. Ibid.
9. Ibid.
10. Judson Edwards, *The Leadership Labyrinth: Negotiating the Paradoxes of Ministry* (Macon, Ga.: Smyth & Helwys, 2005), 4.
11. Bernard Cooke, *Power and the Spirit of God: Toward an Experienced-Based Pneumatology* (New York: Oxford University Press, 2004), 23.
12. Ibid., 40.

13. Richard Robert Osmer, *A Teachable Spirit: Recovering the Teaching Office in the Church* (Louisville: Westminster John Knox, 1990), 141.

14. Cooke, *Power and the Spirit of God*, 141.

15. *Screening in Faith: A National Education Campaign on Screening Resource* (Ottawa: Volunteer Canada, 1999).

16. Ibid., 1.1.

17. David Johnson and Jeff VanVonderen, *The Subtle Power of Spiritual Abuse: Recognizing and Escaping Spiritual Manipulation and False Spiritual Authority within the Church* (Minneapolis: Bethany House, 1991), 13–21.

18. Ibid., 69.

19. Ibid., 79.

20. Ibid., 121.

Chapter 6

1. Reginald E. Y. Wickett, *How to Use the Learning Covenant in Religious Education: Working with Adults* (Birmingham, Ala.: Religious Education Press, 1999), 10.

2. "Guidelines for Developing Ministry Personnel Position Descriptions," August 2003, can be found at http://www.unitedchurch.ca/pastoralrelations/pdf/mppdescriptions.pdf.

3. Erwin Berry, *The Alban Personnel Handbook for Congregations* (Herndon, Va.: Alban Institute, 1999), 77.

4. Ibid., 78–97. Berry also includes all samples on a CD for easy use and adaptation.

5. Ibid., 109.

6. Ibid., viii.

7. Rick Curry, *A Guide to Church Management* (Lima, Ohio: Fairway Press, 2002), 7.

8. Norma deWaal Malefyt and Howard Vanderwell, *Designing Worship Together: Models and Strategies for Worship Planning* (Herndon, Va.: Alban Institute, 2005), 37.

9. Ibid.

10. Berry, *Alban Personnel Handbook for Congregations,* viii.

11. Gilbert R. Rendle, *Leading Change in the Congregation: Spiritual and Organizational Tools for Leaders* (Herndon, Va.: Alban Institute, 1998), 173.

12. These three hymns can be found in a number of hymnals, including *Voices United: The Hymn and Worship Book of the United Church of Canada* (Toronto: The United Church Publishing

House), in which these are hymns 512, 510, and 509, respectively.

Chapter 7

1. Cranton, *Understanding and Promoting Transformative Learning,* 89.
2. Dominice, *Learning from Our Lives,* 161.

Chapter 8

1. Linda J. Vogel, "Reckoning with the Spiritual Lives of Adult Educators," in Leona M. English and Marie Gillen, eds., *Addressing the Spiritual Dimensions of Adult Learning: What Educators Can Do: New Directions for Adult and Continuing Education, No. 85* (San Francisco: Jossey-Bass, 2000), 17.
2. Jane Vella, "Spirited Epistemology: Honoring the Adult Learner as Subject" in *Addressing the Spiritual Dimensions of Adult Learning,* 7.
3. Vogel, "Reckoning with the Spiritual Lives of Adult Educators," 22–23.
4. Leona M. English, "Spiritual Dimensions of Informal Learning" in *Addressing the Spiritual Dimensions of Adult Learning,* 30.